A WAY WITH WORDS

Also by Edward England

An Unfading Vision
The Spirit of Renewal

Other Highland Books

By Paul Tournier
The Adventure of Living
Escape from Loneliness
A Doctor's Casebook in the Light of the Bible
Secrets

By Michael Green
Evangelism in the Early Church

By Edith Schaeffer
What is a Family?

by John L. Sherrill
They Speak with other Tongues.

A Way with Words

A Handbook for Christian Writers

Edited by
EDWARD ENGLAND

HIGHLAND BOOKS

Printed in Great Britain for
HIGHLAND BOOKS
Crowton House, The Broadway, Crowborough, East Sussex TN6 1AB,
by Richard Clay (The Chaucer Press) Ltd, Bungay, Suffolk.
Typeset by Nuprint Services Ltd, Harpenden, Herts.

Contents

Introduction 7

1. Finding the Time   *Marion Stroud*   9
2. Only Write if you 'Have' to!   *Rhena Taylor*   21
3. Writing for Magazines   *Derek Williams*   33
4. Writing for Children   *Jean Watson*   45
5. Writing for Radio   *David Winter*   61
6. Writing in Partnership   *David Phypers*   75
7. Writing for the National Press   *Martyn Halsall*   85
8. Ghost-Writing   *Jane Collins*   97
9. Writing for a Book Publisher   *Robert Warner*   109
10. Do I Need an Agent?   *Edward England* 121
11. How a Writer Sees   *Jenny Cooke*   133
12. Having Something to Say   *Jenny Cooke*   143

Introduction

If you seek this book in a library or bookshop please pronounce the title carefully. It is not *Away with Words*: although there have been times when like most publishers and literary agents I have felt like that. It is *A Way with Words*.

For eighteen years my desk has been swamped, from around the world, with manuscripts. Most have been well-presented, beautifully typed, the fruit of months and sometimes years of labour. A small proportion have been accepted for publication, perhaps one thousand. Most of these books have been moderately successful selling upwards of three thousand as hardbacks or ten thousand as paperbacks. A number have exceeded one hundred thousand, and a handful have passed the half-million mark. This book is not primarily for those authors although all of them would benefit from it.

It is dedicated to the thousands of writers whose manuscripts I have had to reject. I rarely sent them a printed rejection slip but nevertheless had to content myself with three or four paragraphs when I would like to have written at length. There was so much that might have been said. This book is an attempt to say some of those things through the words of contemporary Christian writers whose work is regularly in print.

Personally, I have learned from what they have written. I

am indebted to them. Also to my friend and author Jenny Cooke for preparing the manuscript for the printer.

EDWARD ENGLAND

Crowborough, Sussex
1984

Chapter One

FINDING THE TIME

By

Marion Stroud

'Great men never complain about lack of time. Alexander the Great and John Wesley accomplished everything they did in twenty-four hour days.'

Marion Stroud lives in Bedford with her husband and children. Her two main publishers are Pickering and Inglis and Lion. Most of her books have been published in America and some of her illustrated titles such as *The Gift of Love* and *The Gift of Years* have been translated into several languages. Her latest book is *Women at Prayer*.

'*Great men never complain about lack of time. Alexander the Great and John Wesley accomplished everything they did in twenty-four hour days.*'

'If that is true,' said my friend, gloomily eyeing the poster pinned up over my desk, 'then I don't think that I've ever met any great writers!'

The favourite topic of conversation at our Writers' Circle is the earth-shaking books, stories, articles or epic poems that we would write, could write, and are, in fact, all just burning to write—when we get the time! But our actual output is pitifully small! We seem to be so much better at talking about writing than doing it!

Finding time to write! This seems to be the first major pitfall on the road to success and the one into which many a would-be writer sinks without trace. And if this is a problem for writers in general, then it would seem to be an even bigger potential hazard for Christian writers. After all, committed Christians who are active in their local churches are not noted for having time to spare! When the day's work is done, the needs of one's family dealt with, those inside the church cared for and those outside of it contacted for Christ, what hope is there of finding any *spare* time in which to write?

Of course not all Christian writers are in the same situation—in fact they seem to fall roughly into three groups. The first (and by far the smallest) group are those who are professional journalists, script writers or authors in the same way as one might be a Christian teacher, factory worker or shop-keeper. They will certainly have many problems to face, but finding time to write will not be the major one, because writing is their full-time occupation.

The second group are Christian leaders—usually preachers!—whose spoken word or experiences in Christian work are of sufficient general interest for them to be invited by a magazine editor or book publisher to write them down. They will undoubtedly have problems in finding time to write, but because they have been *asked* to do it, they will probably have less trouble in justifying the finding of that time to themselves and other people.

Then there are the majority of Christian writers. Some of us may have ambitions to become full-time writers eventually; others may simply see their writing as being part of their wider Christian service. In either case, writing has to be fitted in around other commitments, and that is not easy. After sixteen years of fighting the clock I still haven't won the battle completely. But I'm learning. And the most important thing that I have learned is that God has given us enough time to do all the things that *he* wants us to do. My job is to find out what those things are, and then to get on with them.

Is it worth doing anyway?

This is the first question that you have to ask yourself as a writer; if you don't, someone else most certainly will! As one elderly lady said to me (eyeing the waste-paper basket full of scrumpled paper that represented most of my morning's work), 'Do you really feel that you are using God's fleeting moments in the best possible way?'

It is a valid question. The Bible has quite a lot to say about the wise use of our time and our talents. We need to be firmly convinced that what we are doing is right; to have a realistic understanding of what the written word can and cannot achieve, and a vision of how it can help to bring in the Kingdom of God before we can hope to convince other people.

Catch the vision!

The written word can be dynamite! Communism has not been spread principally by its fighting men but by its writing men—most notably Karl Marx, a journalist. Mao held sway in China more because of the influence of his 'little red book' than because of the activities of the Red Guard. And where would Christians be without the Bible? Even in this television and video age, there is still a great need for Christians who can 'write the vision and make it plain', communicating effectively with those outside as well as those within the church. This gift is not given to everyone, and those of us who have been entrusted with it should be very aware of our responsibility to use it well. Remember the servant in the parable who buried the one talent he was given in the ground? He not only missed out on the thrill of achievement but also on his master's commendation. As Tim Stafford says, 'The commitment to excellence requires that we first of all discover our gifts and then invest them with abandonment.' No half-measures!

Identify your talent and your calling

At a recent Writers' Conference I was interested to find that many of the would-be writers to whom I chatted had one thing in common—they didn't really know what they were aiming at. Some vaguely thought that they would like to, 'write for children'; others confessed that they liked to write 'about people' or wanted to 'share their faith with non-Christians' but few had taken the time to establish, through studying the work of others, experimenting in various areas of writing themselves and then accepting informed criticism, where their talents lay. And a surprising number saw no reason why they should expect a period of more failures than successes while they were learning their craft. 'If it is God's will for me to be a writer,' said one individual pompously, 'then I see no reason why he would want me to waste my time writing things that are not going to be published!' When I had recovered my powers of speech I pointed out that if a writer like J. B. Priestley could say, 'Write...not with the idea at once of getting into print but as if you were learning to play an instrument,' then that was good enough for me. In fact I often think that God allowed me to become involved with writing in order to teach me patience!

We also need to grasp the fact that not every writer is going to succeed in every area of the craft. Some will write fiction, others fact. Some have the stamina to write book-length manuscripts, others will be equally effective with short articles. What we do need to know is what we, as individuals, are gifted to do; whether we are one talent writers, whose main field of operation will be for the benefit of the local church or community, or whether we have been endowed with five or even ten talents and should be investing a great deal of time in our work. It is only once we have identified our talents and been assured of our calling that we can begin to grapple with the problem of finding time to write, without the paralysing conflict of interests that leaves so many of us indecisive and ineffectual.

Aim for your goal

All the books that I have read on time management (three of the most useful are listed at the end of the chapter) stress this point: that we need to know what it is we are aiming at, as we set about organising our time. In other words we need to set goals. A goal is not a vague dream but something that is both definable and attainable so that we know what we are trying to do and whether or not we have done it.

In their book *Strategy for Living* Edward Dayton and Ted Engstrom suggest seven positive steps that we can take to translate a goal that seems as far away as the moon into reality.

1. *Understand your purpose*—what is it that you want to happen?
2. *Picture the situation*—what would it be like?
3. *State some long range goals*—what steps would lead to this situation?
4. *State your immediate goals*—what should you do now?
5. *Act*—get on with it.
6. *Act as if*...your goal is within your grasp.
7. *Keep praying*.

Without realising it (not having read the book at the time!) this is just what I did when I 'retired' from physiotherapy to have our first baby. Dazzled with visions of all the free time which I *thought* that I was going to have, I decided that I would fulfil two ambitions at once, and as well as becoming a mother I would become a writer! *This was my purpose*. I certainly *pictured the situation* with rosy dreams of a shelf full of books with my name on the spines! However, I realised that a book might be rather a tall order to start with so with that in mind as a *long range goal*, I tested my talent and calling by starting a correspondence course, and writing some short articles, most of which were published.

Encouraged by this I had another baby and when he was just a few weeks old discovered a competition designed for new writers of children's books. Here was my chance. The timing was hardly ideal, but the competition gave me two invaluable spurs: a specific target at which to aim—not 'a book someday' but 'a children's book for 8-11 year olds'; and a deadline by which to get it done. My long range goal became medium range—a completed manuscript in six months' time. *My immediate goals were:*

1. to devise a way of getting through the chores more rapidly.
2. to enlist the help of my husband.
3. to set aside certain evenings each week on which I could work (while he rocked the baby if necessary!).
4. to get a supply of paper.
5. at the appointed time to sit down and get on with it!

And that is how my dream began to be translated into reality.

Priorities, priorities

Of course while I was writing that book (and ever since) I was still a wife, a mother, and most important of all, a Christian. So although one of my priorities then was to make sure that certain periods of time were kept free to write, another was to make sure that my relationship with God and with my family was not crowded out. And that is *very* important. It is so easy, when we are trying to fit a new activity into an already busy life, for 'the work' to become more important than God himself, and that is a recipe for disaster. The Bible is quite clear. Our first priority is to be our relationship with God—he is more interested in what we are than what we do for him. Our second priority is to be our relationships with others, and then... the writing. As one American writer has put it, 'I am not simply a full-time Christian writer. I am, by God's grace, a full-time Christian who writes. I must go on renewing my mind in the Word of God, if my words are to reveal his mind to others.'

We are responsible for the words we write, and we need to be constantly aware of the impact that those words may have on the lives of others and take that responsibility seriously. A few years ago I went with my parents to view a house that they were thinking of buying for their retirement. To my surprise the vendor was someone I knew slightly, a Christian lady whose marriage to a man who did not share her faith was reputed to be very stormy. As we went round the house I noticed that she had one of my books on her bookshelf; one that I had written for women in her position. I didn't comment but I was saddened to hear her say the house was for sale because she was divorcing her husband. My parents decided against the purchase, and apart from a brief prayer that day I thought no more about it…until I met her a few weeks later. When I enquired whether she had sold the house yet she shook her head. 'I've taken it off the market and stopped my divorce proceedings,' she said. Before I could respond she added, 'When I saw you and remembered what you had written in that book of yours, I knew that I was doing the wrong thing!' I was both speech-less and humbled. The knowledge that God had used my words to have that kind of influence on someone else's life made writing them a terrifying responsibility.

Have you got something to say?

One of the biggest complaints of editors and publishers is not so much that the manuscripts which pour on to their desks are badly written or poorly researched but that they do not say anything that has not been said before. They often answer questions that people were asking twenty years ago. Why? Well, partly because the writer has with-drawn into an ivory tower and lost touch with ordinary people. As Christian writers we must certainly walk closely with God, but we must also be able to say with the prophet Ezekiel, 'I sat where they sat.' We have to be prepared to feel the pain, the fears and the perplexity of a broken world, and that takes time. But time spent listening, reading, discussing and sometimes simply watching, is not time stolen from writing but time invested in it, because it should result in writing that is rooted in reality.

Plan your work and then work your plan

So you know your purpose. You are assured of your calling. You have set your goals and you know what needs to be written. Now comes the tricky part—you have to carve out time in your life to write and then get down to it at the time appointed.

Writing time never just happens. It has to be fought for, and this means streamlining every day living so that you can *make* time. It is certainly true that we can all find time to do what we really want to do, but we may have to learn to write under pressure.

Winston Churchill is reputed to have written 10,000 words of original composition each day, in the heat of the desert and while conducting the affairs of the Second World War. On a more homely level a mother of eight, who had no play-group or nursery school within reach, used to take her three pre-schoolers on a long journey into town by bus so that she could use the facilities of the department store nursery for two hours. She would do her shopping at break-neck speed and then spend the rest of her child-free time in the Ladies Room, getting on with her writing! She also volunteered to look after Sam (who was such a little horror that even his grandmother would not look after him) for a whole day each week in return for three free hours while Sam's mother took charge of her children. Where there's a will there's a way!

It may seem that women who are home-based have much more flexibility in their day-to-day lives and can fit their writing in more easily. Perhaps this is true for there seem to be many more women writing than men. But it is possible for those working full-time outside the home to find time too. George used to leave home for work an hour earlier than he actually needed to. At that time his drive was cut from a maximum of half-an-hour to a minimum of eight minutes because he avoided the rush hour. And so he had an hour in the office before his colleagues came in, when he could write. A town-centre based business man used to go to the Library for his lunch hour three times a week and sit in the silent Study Area to get on with his work. Some people get up early. Others stay up late. We all have to be prepared to exercise self-discipline without which, talent, no matter how promising, will never reach real fulfilment. And we all have to find the pattern that suits us.

With a family of five school-age children, I find that most of my work has to be done during term-time. My normal work-pattern when I am researching or preparing for a book is two whole days and one half-day each week. But once I start the actual writing, I know that I need to bow out of all but the most essential commitments and work flat out for a month or six weeks until the first draft is finished. I also need a deadline to get me started in the first place! Others prefer to maintain a steady if slower pace and find that a deadline only induces panic! Most writers are individualists and no one writing schedule would suit us all, but there are certain things that we all need to do.

1. Make your plans realistic

It is obviously going to be more productive to plan to write for two hours, three times a week, and to do so, than it is to schedule two hours each day and then to get so depressed because you are not achieving it that you end up hardly writing at all. What is more, it is unfair to yourself and your publisher to make promises that you know you cannot hope to fulfil, just to secure a commission or a contract.

2. Remember that you are not working in isolation

When I make out my writing schedule I have to allow for the fact that my publisher or editor will have his schedule too and won't often reply instantly to my ideas or suggestions. This means thinking as much as a year ahead and perhaps working on more than one project at a time if I am not to waste weeks waiting for other busy people to respond.

3. Refuse to make excuses

Most of us will grasp at any excuse to avoid starting work. The only remedy is to choose a definite starting time and let nothing, other than death or disaster, prevent us from starting work at that precise moment. Remember, 'It won't write itself!'

4. Be prepared for battle

Long ago I had the naive idea that if I was doing God's will I ought to be guaranteed an easy ride. Nothing is further from the truth! People *have* misunderstood my reasons for not being available for their particular projects. There have been days when hours of work have ended in the waste paper basket and it has all seemed a total waste of time. There have been occasions when publishers have seemed less than business-like and critics less than fair. But there have also been the shining moments like the occasion on which someone confided, 'That book you wrote has changed the course of my entire life.' Then I know that the early mornings, the late nights and the hectic days have been infinitely worth while and I know that I will go on making time to write what I have seen of God.

Today we have the opportunity and the freedom to write but tomorrow...? Jesus said, 'All of us must quickly carry out the tasks assigned us by the one who sent me, for there is little time left before the night falls and all work comes to an end.' (John 9:4; LB)

Useful books on the subject of time management

Dayton & Engstrom, *Strategy for Living*, Regal Books.
Pat King, *How Do You Find the Time?* Pickering & Inglis.
Alan Lakien, *How to Get Control of Your Time and Your Life*, Signet Books.

Chapter Two

ONLY WRITE IF YOU HAVE TO

By

Rhena Taylor

'A writer needs a skin like a rhinoceros.'

Rhena Taylor is with the Bible Churchman's Missionary Society in Kenya. She has written for television and radio and has published several books, the most recent being *Every Single Blessing* launched by Kingsway Publications in Spring 1984. She has now completed the draft of her first novel *The Missionaries*.

1. On not writing at all

One of the dangers of having written and published, even modestly, is that you will be asked to give your opinion on the nearly-completed manuscript which is in a box at the bottom of the fitted cupboard.

I try my very best not to give that opinion. It is almost equal to selling a car in its ability to lose you your friends.

'I just want to know whether you think I could make a career of writing,' says the earnest would-be author whose first effort has just been published by the Mission Society for whom he or she works (as mine was). 'Please be honest. I really want to know.'

'Oh, I always find it difficult to judge the work of people I know,' I say nervously. 'Couldn't you ask someone else?'

But they insist.

I tell them I honestly don't think they have a gift for writing, and they never speak to me again.

I wonder why writing a book is such an attractive idea to people? Is it that they think instant fame will follow the publication of their first effort? It doesn't. My advice to all would-be writers of books is the same: don't do it unless you must (the same advice I once heard given about getting married).

I am sure, if you are reading this book, that you fully understand that to write a book and to have a book published is just not the same thing. People outside the book world never understand this.

'Oh, you're writing a book. How wonderful! Do let me know when it comes out,' they gush, completely ignoring the often long and agonizing struggle to convince a publisher to be interested in your manuscript and the strong proba- bility that it will also end up in a box at the bottom of the fitted cupboard.

You have to face the fact that, just because you use words competently and everyone likes the bits you publish in the parish magazine and/or your missionary prayer letters, it does not necessarily mean you will be able to write a publishable book. Any more than, because I can play an easy Beethoven sonata and accompany hymn singing on the piano, I would expect to fill the Albert Hall for even one night. The rules are different. I have taught writing for a good many years, mostly in Africa. Often I have found an initial problem with a young student is to help him see the difference between a school essay, or an article for the college magazine, and an article likely to be accepted by a national newspaper.

It is not uncommon, for example, for a student who has had neither experience *nor* any special course in politics to hand me an article called, 'Freedom and Equality needed in the Governments of Africa,' and tell me it is intended for the *Daily Nation*. The article is clearly written, obeys the rules of grammar and punctuation and is full of quite unarguable generalisations. But it will not be accepted by a national newspaper. The rules are different.

The nice 'polite' rules of the local church magazine, missionary magazine, or school/college publication are just not the same as the harder, more realistic and competitive rules of the media-masters of the Twentieth century. In that world, unless you are already a nationally-known figure for some other reason (and most of us aren't) you have to fight your way onto the platform of publication. I use the word 'fight' deliberately. You need to be prepared for a few wounds.

Maybe I should make clear at this point that I am not now talking to people who write books on computer programming, travelling to outer Mongolia, or the language of Ethiopia. These are perfectly valid forms of writing and such books, if written by Christians, would come under my definition of 'Christian writing'. But I think people like that have their own armour.

I *am* talking to people who like words and who find themselves basically wanting to share their experiences and insight on Christian living with others through the medium of the written word. It is they who might find themselves with a few wounds on the way to getting into print.

One of our problems is that most of us are quite certain that our experiences or our opinions on life are unique and everyone else is bound to be fascinated by them. It is hard to realise that that isn't so, especially as our friends who read the manuscript assure us that they just 'couldn't put it down'. But to get into print for the popular market today, we really need to have had quite exceptional experiences ('I was a white slave for Idi Amin') or we have to find a completely fresh way of setting them down.

For many years I edited a Christian magazine in Addis Ababa. It was common for us to print testimonies from time to time and a constant stream of young people would bring their written testimonies to us, sure that we would want to publish them. I never *quite* got to the stage of growling, 'Only testimonies involving violence, prison sentences, or sensational miracles will be accepted,' because I felt ashamed that it was so. But I often felt like this!

Another problem is that many people do not always recognise that writing is a craft that does have certain rules attached to it. Sometimes people who would never dream of starting to paint a picture, play a violin, or audition for a part in the West End without at least some training, will start to write a book without giving the technique of writing a thought.

Three of the most useful things I did before I disappeared

to Africa were learning to type, teaching English grammar in a secondary school (and thus learning how to punctuate direct speech), and taking a correspondence course in short story writing. Writers might be 'born and not made'—in fact I incline to think they are—but they can still learn a lot from consciously studying the writers' craft and learning where their particular strengths and weaknesses are.

Yes, getting into print is not easy but, even if we don't manage to fill the Albert Hall, we can still enjoy playing the piano! A lot can be done by the person who likes writing even if their chief masterpiece remains in the box at the bottom of the fitted cupboard.

When I start a writing class I often write my definition of good writing on the blackboard: GOOD WRITING IS WRITING THAT IS READ. And by that I mean, read by the people you intend to read it. Not many writers write for themselves (although I acknowledge the therapeutic value of the diary or the emotion-packed poem); most write to communicate. And communication falls pretty flat if it doesn't even reach the person it's intended for. If your writing isn't *read* then it is not good writing.

If you write for the parish magazine, and if people really read what you've written, which is more than I can say for the article at the start which ends 'your sincere friend and vicar', then that is good writing. If you write a missionary prayer letter that actually gets beyond being tucked under the Bible for later perusal, then that is good writing. I don't think you need to consider how *many* people actually read what you've written. If your writing is being read by the people you meant to read it, then you are a successful writer!

In fact you can get a lot of fun from writing on the local level: letters to the local paper, a play for your church to perform, a poem to go on the general invitation to the harvest supper, a dramatic Bible reading for the youth club and so on. I have a feeling there are lots of humbler things not written at all because those who could write them still have their eyes fixed on that knock-'em-all-for-six novel.

2. On where to start if you must.

OK. So you've read all I said in the last section and you still want to head for the stars. You still have the basic question inside you, 'could I be a successful writer?' One way of finding an answer to that question is to ask yourself, 'How much do I actually *write*?'

I think true writers will usually write, whether anyone is asking them to or not. They see things: scenes, emotions, situations, in terms of words and will incline to jot them down somewhere sometime. 'You learn to write by writing' is another of those trite aphorisms that I inflict on my classes but I think it is true. If you haven't already been writing then I should doubt your sudden urge to start writing a book.

Of course there are 'one book' people. Something special happens and they want to share it. They write themselves or sometimes get a known writer to help them and there they are. An author. Such books are often much blessed with high sales but when the gratified author decides to write another, ('that one was so easy. It practically wrote itself'), he finds to his surprise that it isn't as easy as that. Books come from a desire to communicate something to someone: not from a desire to write a book.

Recently a friend in the USA sent me a manuscript he was thinking of publishing. He had written in the foreword: 'Mrs. X. didn't really want to write this book but while I was in her office I saw all the material she had and persuaded her to agree to put it together in a book.'

I think this is bad psychology. When I pick up a book to read I want to read something the author really wants me to know: even if it is only how to look after my pot plants. If I'm going to feel, right at the start, that in fact she *didn't* specially want to tell me what was in the book, then I lose some of my interest. Do we like to be talked to by someone who doesn't want to talk to us? Do we like to feel that unimportant to the writer?

So, before you start on your book, check that you really have something to *say*. It isn't enough to say 'I want to write my life story' or 'I want to write down my views on adult baptism in the Anglican church': you must say 'I want to say *that* to *those people* in order that they ...' Let us talk for a moment about the people you are writing for: your target audience. Don't forget about them. You are not writing for *Family* magazine, or *Readers' Digest*, or your chosen book publisher. You are writing for the people who will read what you have written.

I often teach courses in Communication Theory and a lot of my teaching material involves being 'receptor oriented': really thinking about and becoming closely involved with your 'target audience'. We must not ignore them, look down on them, feel sorry for them or patronize them. They are really the centre of any communication act: which includes the writing of a book. You will never make a successful writer if you relate badly to people. People are your stock-in-trade. It is by knowing them, their interests, needs, activities and life-styles that you will be enabled to write something they will read.

'I'm longing to make enough money to retire to Sicily and write books for a living,' said a friend of mine recently who works in computers in Central London. But I wonder if that would work. For a writer to cut himself off from people is to lose the raw material of which books are made.

I notice in the missionary world that, sometimes, it is the people who are finding it difficult to live in the strains and tensions of cross-cultural relationships that often get assigned to 'literature work'. They shut the door thankfully on that busy and confusing outer world and retire into writing books, or translating the Bible or whatever. But the mass media (of which print is one) is merely an extension of our communicatory powers. In other words, if we aren't making it on a one-to-one basis then it is unlikely we will make it in the literature ministry.

3. On finding the right publisher

So you have your message, your 'target audience' and you know something of what you want to achieve. Now to find the right publisher or, if you are thinking of an article, the right editor.

You have to do some homework here so that you don't:

—offer fiction to a magazine that only deals in theological articles.

—offer an article critical of the charismatic movement to a magazine funded by Pentecostals.

—offer a book on the prophecies of Daniel to a publisher who likes light romances.

—offer a 2000-word article to a newspaper which only deals in 400-word articles. And so on. Take advice, study the market, talk your idea over with editors, or write telling them what the idea is, and try *not* to write a 50,000 word book and post it without any word of warning to your favourite publisher!

Publishers on the whole are on the look-out for new authors and are unlikely to totally discourage you right at the start, unless they feel the idea is really hopeless. They may write something like, 'It is possible we would be interested in an article on the topic you mention if it is interestingly written and demonstrates a fresh approach to the subject. However it is only fair to warn you that we only very rarely publish unsolicited manuscripts.'

I should not finish this section without mentioning the need of living with rejections. A friend of mine from Canada, who has published a fair amount, recently said, 'You know, Rhena, I've never had a rejection slip'. I didn't tell her at the time but our friendship has never been nearer extinction than it was at that moment. I dare say there are writers who never experience rejection but I'd rather not know about them.

We have to live with rejections if we are going to make it as writers. I wish I'd made a collection of mine. I think the best one I had said something like, 'the plot is weak, the characters flat and uninteresting and the dialogue boring'. It stings to this day! But fortunately most publishers are a lot kinder than that and simply write, 'It is not what we are in need of at the moment'. We have to tell ourselves firmly that the publisher or editor is not thinking, 'what a weak and futile writer must have written this manuscript' but 'this is a manuscript I cannot use' and learn to take it back with some degree of detachment.

We can learn from rejections: sometimes editors will offer helpful comments on them. But the important thing is, we must not let them paralyse us. Keep remembering those nice stories about famous writers that had publisher after publisher reject their manuscripts before they were finally accepted: and turn such phrases as 'boring dialogue' or 'uninteresting characters' out of your mind.

4. On surviving once you have started

When you have had a few things published and have come to terms with the fact that they have not made you famous overnight and that some of your friends have not even bothered to buy your book, you may realise that one of the things a Christian writer has to come to terms with is a disinclination to write.

I haven't checked this out with others but I know myself that the minute I sit down to write something at the typewriter, I find I want to go to the bathroom or need a cup of tea or see a cobweb in the corner I'd never noticed before. Then the phone rings. Of course that isn't exactly my fault, but I needn't have talked for half an hour. Somehow, just anything appears more attractive than starting to write. I don't know if this is a Satan-directed campaign, which he puts into operation immediately he sees a Christian with a good idea for a book. But I do know it happens every time.

So much for the idea that writers seize the typewriter with a gladsome cry and set off with the light of inspiration on their brows. If you're going to wait for that, you'll wait for ever.

We are, I think, naturally quite lazy. There are so many different types of writing but some are more work than others and we tend to opt for the ones with less work attached.

I notice that in the publication we have in my own local church. It is a publication basically intended for church news. But church news takes time to collect. You have to attend functions; you have to find the right people to interview whose schedule never fits yours; you have to hang around in order to report a speech given much later than you had thought. News is what people want. News is what will sell the paper. But news is hard to collect and takes time and patience. So what happens? The minute I leave on holiday the paper gets full of 'devotional articles' or 'the Vicar's sermon on the Second Coming'. More church magazines die because of filling them with the Vicar's sermon than for any other single cause! But we still prefer to write a devotional piece in our study bedrooms than we do to get out there and write what people want to read.

Then there is the matter of criticism. 'Writing is Risking,' says another book. There's a lot of truth in that. You publish something you've really worked hard on and find within the next few weeks that:

—Mr and Mrs W. are really quite horrified at the remarks you made about the Presbyterians.
—Mr C. feels you should have tackled the whole thing from another angle.
—You have got Mrs Pottsliger's initials wrong.
—The Vicar is very upset because you didn't discuss the manuscript with him before publication.
—Miss E. thinks the cover of the book would put anyone off right at the start.

The flood of appreciative letters which you expected just didn't arrive.

A writer needs a skin like a rhinoceros.

But keep writing. It has its good moments as well as its bad ones: like finishing a manuscript that's been haunting you for months. Like this one.

Chapter Three

WRITING FOR MAGAZINES

By

Derek Williams

The success of a magazine article begins with the first sentence...

Derek Williams was editor of *Third Way* from 1977–1978, and *Today* (formerly *Crusade*) from 1980–1983. He is also the author of *About People* (IVP) and *Handbook of Christian Living* (Scripture Union).

'The success of a magazine article begins with the first sentence . . .'

'The editor has asked me to produce a model article showing you how to do it; this I have endeavoured to do in five sections.'

Forget it! You've bored your reader into turning over. You sound pompous, too, when in reality you're hacking it out on the dining room table after a hard day, with the telly blaring in one ear and the goldfish blowing bubbles in the other. Start again.

'Many are penpushers but few are writers.' True, clever, and quite useless as a starter. Don't mystify your reader; grab him. You're competing with a bunch of other articles; stop him flipping on to the next one. Once more.

'Many unsolicited articles sent to magazines are incoherent, irrelevant and uninteresting.' Much better! It's startling, provocative and sadly true. You may just have persuaded the reader who thinks he's the finest pen in the west to settle down for a bit of cosy criticism of Other People. (Easy to write, but what good does it do?) More likely, he's concluding you are just another sadistic editor armed with rejection slips and chocolate-coated fingers who's about to turn his impeccable ms into a crumpled mess. You're negative—do something quick to keep him.

'Many authors could save themselves the heartbreak of seeing their hard work rejected if they followed a few simple rules.' Well done! You've gone straight to the point. And you're not getting at him after all—you're his friend, with some useful tips he needs to know! Look, he's settling into the chair, crossing his legs, even taking his finger out of the contents page.

So off you go. Tell him simply, clearly and humanly. Add a dash of humour, a splash of colour, and give it lots of pace...

Motives: what's your game?

No editor will publish an article without a good reason. So the writer needs one too. Pin money is not a good reason. What you will earn from Christian periodicals will buy nothing but a hatful of pins. Besides, your talents deserve a better excuse for their exercise. And the selfish streak will almost certainly be noticed by the discerning reader.

Perhaps you feel strongly about something. Show me a person without strong feelings and I will show you a corpse! You need more than concern to avoid the editor's out-tray; you need carefully researched facts and a fresh presentation. Some authors dash off an article in response to one that has annoyed them, but end up writing only an unpublishable (because it is too long) letter to the editor. The heat of passion may be fine in the pulpit but it is folly on paper.

Of course, you may just enjoy writing. Personally, I find it hard work; the real satisfaction comes when the last word is polished to perfection, which is a long time after the first word was scribbled. However, not every clever combination of words makes a printable feature. You need to have something new to say, and you will have to work hard at saying it in a limited space. Anyone can ramble, but only the fit can sprint.

And just in case there is a vestige of glamour remaining in the idea of being published in a magazine, remember what you ate your chips out of last night, and what is currently lining your kitchen bin. Magazines are laboriously produced and quickly forgotten.

Rule one is: Think before you write. 'Search me, O God, and know my heart . . . See if there is any offensive way in me.'

Mindset: What's your poison?

The writer's mindset is not the essential trilogy of dictionary, thesaurus and concordance. It is a contemporary cliché for the way you think about things. Which may not be how others think. Some writers wax eloquent but totally fail to communicate. An exercise in sharing becomes an essay of self-expression. What is meat to them becomes poison to the reader.

We can become so wrapped up in our ideas or experiences, so convinced that others must, this very hour, make the same grand discoveries, appropriate the same life-changing truths, that we forget all about the reader, that long-suffering person who has never heard of us, whose ideas are starkly different to ours and which are coloured by experiences we have never dreamed of, and who is strangely unmoved by our purple prose . . .

'I do like the cartoons that Taffy does.'

'Ready for your tea, now, Doris?'

'Is it that late already?'

Poor Doris! She left school at fourteen, has varicose veins and a non-Christian husband.

Show yourself careless, or even contemptuous, of her and you will not get through to her. If you beat her, she will leave you and find some other author to love. If you bamboozle her, she will avoid you like the plague when next you turn up on her doormat.

It may all be self-evident to you. Your information may be accurate, and your judgment perfect. Your storyline may be riveting and your literary construction heading straight for the Booker Prize. But right now Doris's leg aches and she fancies tea more than theology.

Rule two is: Words are written by the people for the people. 'A farmer went out to sow his seed . . . Some fell on rocky places, where it did not have much soil.'

Market: who are you getting at?

For four years I edited a national magazine which carried one 'devotional' feature every month, usually written by one of a small team of well-known Bible teachers or evangelists. And what did Aspiring Author of Bognor send me? Devotional articles. It makes you wonder if some writers can read.

Gone are the days when G. K. Chesterton could advocate writing articles for journals politically on the far left and far right, and deliberately posting them in the wrong envelopes. In the Christian market there is surprisingly little overlap between magazines; they each have an identifiable emphasis, readership and style. Even secular magazines are not nearly so alike as the rows of similar titles on the shelves may suggest.

So if you want to write especially for *Fuzz* or *Christian He-man*, get hold of as many back copies as you can, and analyse them. What sort of feature do they carry regularly? How are topics dealt with? What level and length are they written at? What is the general style and approach, and what is the likely readership? Are some slots covered by regular contributors (and therefore closed to outsiders)? Have they covered your subject recently? If so, try somewhere else! A monthly magazine with twelve issues and perhaps forty-eight main articles a year is not going to repeat subjects very often. When you have done your research, gear your article to suit the precise requirements of your intended outlet. And if that editor rejects it, think about revamping it before trying it elsewhere.

Space in the national magazines is limited. But there is a whole host of local magazines which some writers quite wrongly despise. Every church has one. Their editors are often desperate for quality material to add variety to the flower rota and the list of burials. Their readers will probably never see another Christian journal. You will get no fee from them on earth. But you just might find your words preserved in a nugget of gold in heaven.

Rule three is: Fire your arrows at a specific target. 'I have become all things to all men so that by all possible means I might save some.'

Matter: What are you saying?

Most magazines articles can be slotted into one of four categories. Each one needs a different approach. Each has its *own* hidden traps to ensnare the unwary writer; each has its own strengths and values.

1. Profiles: the human touch

Whether or not it is a good thing, the most popular and remembered articles (and books and TV programmes and even conversations) are about people. An obvious reason is that people identify more readily with fellow humans than with abstract concepts. Some writers, however, prefer ideas. They are predictable, and amenable to the scientific mind-set. People merely confuse issues by changing their minds.

Another reason for the popularity of human stories is the voyeurism which likes peering into other people's houses when the lights are on and the curtains open. And a third is the vicarious excitement colourful characters can bring to our own dull, common or garden existence.

The fact that public figures can be bled dry by the leech-like press is no reason for not writing and publishing personal profiles. But it does demand that Christian writers and editors approach them carefully.

For example, I published the first Christian magazine interview with tennis player Sue Barker after she had become a Christian. There was a gentleman's agreement that she would be kept out of the Christian limelight until she was well-established in the faith. But so much nonsense was circulating in the secular press that we felt a responsibility to set the record straight. It is amazing how many Christians believe what they read in the gossip columns! We had to be sure we did not sensationalise it, but tell her story soberly yet attractively.

Another which required sensitive handling was an interview with TV botanist David Bellamy. He had a strong Christian background and deep concerns about matters which many Christians had long ignored. He spoke freely of his lack of a 'Damascus Road' experience advocated in his boyhood church.

We made little comment about his views. Start editorialising or apologising and you ruin an article and offend your subject. But we wanted the feature to make non-Christians think about the existence of God, and evangelicals to think about their insistence on a certain kind of experience of God. And to encourage readers to pray for a public figure whenever they saw him on their screens.

Before you begin a profile, ask what is unique about this person's life or experience. You need to strike a chord of interest in the readers. If the subject is a public personality, that may be reason enough. Or, they may have unique insights into some area of human experience which others can learn from.

I once carried an interview with an otherwise unknown person who happened to head up the Customs drugs investigators at Heathrow Airport. He could share things no one else could. But the patience of Doris with her varicose veins, while making a short filler for a local newsletter, will never hit the headlines.

Then, do your homework. Find out all you can about the person from books or other people. Familiarise yourself with their special interest. Draw up a list of questions to direct your conversation with them. Beware the professionals; Malcolm Muggeridge once *answered* all my questions and left me groping for more after fifteen minutes of a scheduled forty-five minute interview! Decide in advance to focus on one aspect of their life, or outline all of it—but never both.

Make an appointment to see them. Never write profiles based on hearsay or press reports. Errors and emphases soon turn into judgments and rumours. Use a taperecorder rather than taking notes, as rapid writing will destroy any sense of conversation. A taperecorder also guarantees accuracy.

Always look for 'colour'—mannerisms, personality, the home or environment. You will not necessarily describe these in detail, but an occasional aside or even a choice adjective will help convey the subject's humanness.

Make sure you understand the chronology of their story, but never write it like a diary. You must give your reader adequate reference points, otherwise you will lose him in a maze of detours.

Be neither pretentious nor coy. Your assessments are not to be paraded (the feature is not about *you*), but neither are they to be hidden. Your very selection of material and approach is itself an assessment. The simple verbatim interview rarely works unless you have a very crisp speaker across the table. Your task is to paint a word picture which will include the subject's own statements and your précis of their life or view.

Tell it straight; turn your subject into neither a saint nor a sensation. If the story is praiseworthy, the reader does not have to be told.

Rule four is: Be honest and illuminating without glamourising or horrifying. 'The truth will set you free.'

2. Topical debates: cooling the heat

Articles on topical subjects can be the undoing of both the experts who create them and the writers who unpack them. They need all the journalist's armoury.

A single word captures the aim: *comprehension*. Does the author really comprehend all the sides of the argument, or is he writing a thinly-veiled piece of propaganda? Will the reader gain a fresh comprehension of the discussion and the issues involved, or will he conclude you are just another barrack-room bigot?

Even if something is as clear-cut as, say, euthanasia, you should show yourself aware of other views, even if you do not refer to them directly. What is the point of a Christian feature condemning euthanasia if the author shows no feeling for people worn down by dependant, geriatric relatives? Christian matters should reflect a Christian mind.

There are no short cuts to research, even if the deadline is pressing. Select and read the main books or papers. If the article is more than a brief summary, phone or visit some experts. Discuss with neighbours or friends what the real issues are and how they affect ordinary people. Then meditate on the issues before rushing into print. Use quotations from others sparingly. Your aim is to illustrate a subject, not preach a sermon or give a lecture.

Some magazines will want you to break down the material into bite-size chunks, which the designers will separate out into visually more appealing 'boxes'. You will need to be logical and systematic (which does not mean dull or pedantic).

Avoid assuming prior knowledge but at the same time do not treat your reader as if he were an idiot from another planet. Find common phrases to replace technical language. Keep the style as racy and colourful as you would a profile. You will have to work hard at this; your reader would prefer to read about Doris than death, unless he happens to be an undertaker. But avoid the crudity of statements like, 'It could be your machine they switch off.'

Rule five is: Create more light than heat; truth is not served by propaganda. 'Walk in the light, as he is in the light.'

3. Devotional features: pointing to God

Old sermons make bad articles; they are as appetising as yesterday's Yorkshire pud. The verbal and written styles are utterly different; pulpit and paper are different media, just as custard and gravy are different sauces.

Devotional features are surprisingly hard to write. They must spring from a close, fresh and living relationship with Christ. And as literature, they must avoid clichés and precious language like the plague. God's truth is worth writing intelligibly. It should not confirm prejudice or wrap people in warm catchphrases.

It is also worth writing practically. Doris must know at once that your ideas can affect her where she is, and are not pious platitudes for mystics. But be subtle. Many devotional features hover in the heavens and never touch earth, but you will best bring them to earth with an almost indefinable quality of empathy rather than forcibly tying them to the kitchen sink.

And remember that a brief filler is sometimes more effective than the thought laboured *ad nauseam*. Let the Spirit apply principles in detail; he will do it better than any writer!

Rule six is: Cut the pie to find the fruit. 'God is in heaven and you are on earth, so let your words be few.'

Method: How will you tackle it?

Every writer has their own way of moving from idea to manuscript. Some work on scraps of paper (that's me!). Others use the typewriter almost exclusively. But whatever your method, you will need to keep some practicalities in mind.

1. Preliminaries

A letter or phone call to an editor outlining your idea could save you the anguish of wasted time. If he likes the idea, he can brief you about his precise requirements. If he rejects it, you can try it on someone else from scratch.

But if no-one wants to publish it (not even the church magazine), still write it. Publication is not the pinnacle of human achievement. Getting your thoughts straight is more important; God wants his people to be clear sighted.

Assuming you have done all your homework and written your draft, you may need to check quotes with the sources, especially if they have come over the phone. Experts are naturally concerned not to be misquoted or to have their comments taken out of context.

2. *Presentation*

Do your polishing in rough, before typing. Use short sentences and paragraphs, simple but varied vocabulary, and watch your spelling. Aim to write naturally but also concisely. Study the average minister's letter in a church magazine for examples of what to avoid!

Normally, you should never address the reader directly. This chapter has been written in the second person because it is a practical 'how to' feature—about the only exception to the rule.

You should not normally use abbreviated words—don't, you're, and even etc. I did at the beginning, in a simulated conversation. It is a stylistic variant to be employed sparingly. Check the magazine for style regarding double or single quote marks and the like.

Follow the usual rules for typing—double spacing, wide left hand margin. Many magazines prefer lines of no more than 36 characters. Always enclose a self-addressed, stamped envelope unless the article has been specially commissioned. Otherwise old chocolate fingers will consign it to the council paper shredder. Give him a few weeks to read your piece before starting your irate phone calls; he is a busy person.

3. *Procedures*

Once accepted, your article will be subject to surgery. This is called sub-editing, preparing the script for press, with some stylistic or grammatical changes to suit the publication. I always let editors do what they like with my prose, in the belief that if they can make it better, I am the winner. (So long as I get the full fee!)

Headlines, cross heads and illustrations are their prerogative too, and will depend on what else is in that issue.

Warning: running over length may endanger your tail. With modern phototypesetting, superfluous paragraphs are literally cut from the artwork with a surgical instrument—a scalpel. If you dislike pain, avoid it.

Rule seven is: Pay attention to detail. 'By your words you will be acquitted and by your words you will be condemned.'

Meanwhile, down at the conclusion, a problem has arisen. More advice? A neat epithet? A terse summary? The scalpel is poised, quivering expectantly.

'I'll have my tea now, dear. Has the news started?'

Ouch.

Bible quotations are from the NIV.

Chapter Four

WRITING FOR CHILDREN

By

Jean Watson

'Brave new life, brave new world.'

Jean Watson lives with her family in Sevenoaks, Kent, and during her children's absence at school writes for a variety of publishers including Hodder and Stoughton, Lion, Kingsway and Scripture Union. In addition to her popular books for children and adults she is a TV scriptwriter and has written for BBC *Playschool*, *Listen with Mother* and Scripture Union's *Sound and Vision*.

Some people think that writing for children, particularly younger ones, is for beginners or those who have failed to make the grade writing for older folk. If you are of that opinion, I hope that you will read on and change your mind! Writing for young children is *at least* as hard to do well as any other form of writing and it requires specialist knowledge and particular skills.

Before enlarging on that statement, I'd like to look at the practical possibilities for the would-be writer, and I see no reason for limiting these to the Christian publishing scene. There is a great need for writers whose human and spiritual lives are so synthesised that *everything* speaks to them of God and his ways; and for such writers to learn the skills and meet the requirements demanded by secular publishing— and not *only* in order to write RE text books, assembly and other 'religious' material. Someone has said, 'History is his story, if a man can climb high enough to read it.' The same could be said of Science, Geography, Social Studies or any other 'subject'. A Christian writer in these fields will not be able to convey overt Christian messages through what he writes, but his viewpoint is bound to make a difference to what he says and how he says it; and 'cool' communication can gently and subtly prepare people for the 'hot' message at the right time.

So what are the possibilities for the writer for young children in the present publishing scene?

Picture books for the very young

Christian and other publishers produce a wide range of picture books for the very young, containing information or stories about people, real or imaginary, and set in the past, present, or—possibly—the future. From Christian publishers come books of prayers, activities or stories (Bible-based or Bible-related) or combinations of these.

Writers would normally be commissioned by a publisher and work closely with an illustrator acceptable to or chosen by him. They would need to have a genuine sympathy with and knowledge of the young child and his world and write suitably for him. I believe this would involve setting the story in the child's world or bridging the gap between his world and the world of the story skilfully and firmly, creating heroes—whether these are toys, animals, machines, magical beings or humans—whom the child will like and identify quickly with, and weaving stories which end safely, happily or satisfactorily.

Any would-be writer ought to take a good, long look at what is already published in this field. The good picture book is one in which the text and the pictures complement and extend rather than duplicate each other, and the skilful writer one who can use nouns and verbs, particularly, to good effect. Through these she can name what needs to be named and convey the action, while the pictures will supply the adjectives, adverbs and atmosphere. For example, if the text reads, 'Jenny unwrapped the present,' the picture could show what Jenny looked like (tall, red-haired, brown-skirted), how she unwrapped the present, (slowly, quickly, gently), and what she felt like (sulky, excited, impatient).

Short stories in anthologies and annuals

Some publishers occasionally accept unsolicited short stories or rhymes for inclusion in annuals and anthologies but you might waste a great deal of postage trying and perhaps failing to find ones that happen to be looking for such material.

Here again, the writer needs to know the child and write within his capabilities. Since there are likely to be fewer pictures, the text has to stand up on its own; so as well as understanding the power of nouns and verbs, an economical use of adjectives and adverbs will be required.

Scripted stories, poems and rhymes for radio and television

Some radio and TV programmes for young children accept freelance material. You would need to listen or watch closely to get the feel of what might be wanted. Then you could try sending in ideas or a story, rhyme or poem, giving relevant details about yourself. There are subtle differences between writing material that is to be spoken by a presenter and that which is for a written medium. The real skill lies in writing a story which will sound as if the presenter is 'adlibbing', even if she is in fact reading, or reciting from memory, every word.

Being aware of the sound of words and learning to use them to good effect are essential for would-be scriptwriters. So are persistence and a sense of call, since radio and television are very hard markets to break into. But anyone who can blow fresh life into these rather enclosed worlds is doing viewers and listeners a service; and Christians particularly could add 'salt' and shed 'light' here.

Stories for primaries and juniors

Christian and other publishers produce books for home and school use in these age ranges. A story written for a secular publisher may differ in content or tone from one written for a Christian one, but it ought to be possible to write good fiction for both markets.

It is harder to define good fiction than to recognise it, I

believe. We need to read currently popular fiction for these age ranges and established classics with a view to discerning between the poor, the mediocre, the adequate, the good and the best. Books critically appraising children's stories can be illuminating here. With their help, try to discover what marks out some children's stories as *literature*.

A few pointers on characterisation, setting, plot and description might help the would-be author for primaries and juniors.

1. Characterisation

The creating (or recreating) of real, rounded characters is enormously important and requires hard work, perception and skill. In some examples of poor fiction, you will find large casts, indistinguishable from one another in the way they think, speak and act, or stereotypes such as jolly policemen, bossy teachers and absent-minded professors. In good fiction, there may not be many characters, but they will all be well-drawn and distinctive; and the skilful writer has no need to *describe* what each person is like, he will *show* it through what his character says, thinks and does.

In view of our young readership, we should create good and likeable, but not perfect, heroes. They should have ordinary human failings, like the rest of us, and why not also, in some cases, physical or mental imperfections? While drawing the line at portraying harrowing disabilities, we mustn't exclude every sort of handicap. Very few heroines even wear spectacles, let alone having to cope with anything more formidable!

Villians should be bad, but not hopelessly wicked. And not funny, either. I am not happy when I see bad behaviour made to look amusing; common to man, and forgiveable, certainly—but not something to laugh at or make light of.

2. Settings

It is still necessary to relate what we write to the child and his world. One way of doing this is to set the action *in* his world. If, as with Bible stories, and tales of other lands or ages, the setting is not the child's world, the writer needs to build bridges between it and the world he is writing about. A time machine is an obvious bridge or device. But equally effective is good characterisation. If the reader can identify with the characters, particularly the hero, he shouldn't find it too difficult to accept the differences as far as speech, dress and background are concerned.

3. Plots

These need to be exciting and credible. The latter word does not imply that fantasy is forbidden. Myth can be a very effective way of conveying truth! But the way we handle the 'magical' elements in our stories will determine whether they are to be taken seriously or not.

Fantasy works best within certain limitations. It should, I believe, spring out of everyday life and ordinary things (as in the Narnia stories where the entrance to the 'other' world lies at the back of a seemingly ordinary, though particular, wardrobe) and the writer must beware of going 'over the top'. One author has suggested that the would-be fantasy writer should allow himself in each story 'no more than one thumping lie'. Certainly, if all problems can be solved with a mere twitch of a nose or wave of a wand, there is no real conflict and character becomes unimportant, and without those two, a story is likely to be weak indeed.

Many writers assume that fantasy is an easy—or perhaps the only—form of writing for young children. They are wrong. I have the feeling that editors would welcome writers who take instead the stuff of ordinary everyday life seen from the child's viewpoint and weave something of worth and meaning from it. Christian writers, if no others, *ought* to have something to offer along these lines. We should never be content merely to cry out, as so many are doing, 'What a mess!' Our job is to proclaim, overtly and subtly, '*This* has meaning!' On the subject of meaning, Paul Tournier has something helpful to say: 'The meaning of life, its total meaning, which imparts to it its unity, despite the diversity of its various stages, is obedience to God.'

4. Description

Long, descriptive passages slow down the narrative and lose the attention of young readers. Adjectives and adverbs are important to convey atmosphere and add subtle touches, but they can be overused.

You might like to try going through some of your work, crossing out all unnecessary words. It's probable that you will discover that you can dispense with a good many adjectives and that you can convey the way some things are said or done through using more precise verbs and omitting the adverbs. For example, if you have written 'grassy lawn', you can cross out 'grassy' since 'lawn' conveys 'grassy' to the reader. If you want the reader to stop and notice the lawn, it will be to draw his attention to the fact that it is close-cropped, overgrown, parched, or whatever.

Similarly, you might be able to replace 'said triumphantly' with 'gloated', or 'walked quickly' by 'strode' or 'hurried' (whichever you really mean).

To write good description we need to cultivate an 'eye' for detail: just enough detail to particularise the table, chair, tree or whatever you want the reader to 'see', or to convey the atmosphere.

Poetry and rhyme

Poetry should not be confused with rhyme or verse written to teach children or help them to remember something. The latter comes under didactic writing. Poetry is creative writing. It could be a very effective means of celebrating or sharing an insight into some truth, but unfortunately there is almost no market for it. Only occasionally will you find picture books for the young in which the text is in rhyme or in a poetic form rather than in prose.

The poems which seem to work best with young children are those with strong, clear themes and a style to match, including imagery which appeals directly to the imagination through the senses, and is bright and sharp. As an example of the latter, consider William Blake's vivid, concrete metaphor: 'Tiger, tiger, burning bright.'

Writing poetry, whether it reaches publication or not, is a good discipline as it forces one to use words precisely and economically and to be aware of their sounds and rhythms.

Bible reading notes and lesson outlines for Sunday School Magazines

Some Christian publishers do use 'outside' writers to contribute to these productions. They would only be prepared to commission people with the relevant teaching, writing and theological qualifications. It would be important, before approaching such publishers, to study what they are producing in this area. If you feel you could contribute, then write giving appropriate details about yourself.

Bible stories, books of prayers and other devotional books for primaries and juniors

As well as producing these sorts of books for the very young, Christian publishers offer a range of them to older children. Obviously, they contain more text and fewer pictures. You will need to study what is being produced and contact the relevant publishers. Writing in with your ideas and sample material, plus relevant details about yourself, would be the sensible first move.

Informative books for primaries and juniors

Some Christian publishers do produce a certain amount of educational material for primaries and juniors, particularly on topics such as the world about us, but the bulk of it comes from other publishers. A writer would need to be commissioned for such work and requirements would be writing skills, experience with children and knowledge of the relevant subject.

It will be obvious even from this brief survey that different kinds of writing are open to the would-be author. We could call these *didactic*, *persuasive* and *creative*. *Didactic* writing covers education, informative material, including Sunday School lesson notes, Bible reading notes (in part), books on the background to the Bible, and 'potted' biographies, written largely in reported style. *Persuasive* writing will be more evident in Bible reading notes—and most devotional material will come into this category. *Creative* writing includes poetry and some stories and biographies (i.e. those in which the writer creates or recreates life through character, dialogue, action, etc.).

Didactic writing usually comes in the form of clear, interesting prose written in an unemotional, impersonal style. The writer needs to understand the child and convey the subject to him in such a way that he will comprehend and learn something from it. His primary aim is to instruct and inform.

Persuasive writing, which is more personal and emotional in tone, can come in the form of prose pieces, stories or verse written to convey the truth more enticingly, the writer's aim being to change his reader's viewpoint, beliefs or behaviour. He must, however, respect the child's freedom and vulnerable emotions and avoid all brainwashing techniques.

Creative writing is also personal and emotional but the writer's intention and style will be different. He will want, primarily to *share* some aspect of truth with his reader through the poem or story he has created, and his influence, if he has any, will be less direct. Ivan Southall has written, 'I am not interested in preaching sermons to children, nor am I trying to house-train children, or to improve them. If quietly, on the side, or round by the back door, or by

53

accident, I help them to grow a little, that's a different matter.'

As Christians, we might not feel it necessary to protest that we are *not* do-gooders, since that, in the right sense, is precisely what we should be. We might also want to be more precise about how we want to help children to grow (i.e. kinder and wiser—not harder and more selfish). Ivan Southall's point is worth noting, nonetheless.

All good, worthwhile writing is about truth or reality in some aspect or other, and involves craftsmanship. The form and style of our writing i.e. *how* we write about the truth, requires its own kind of craftsmanship. There is no space here to say more about these different kinds of craftsmanship, but the following six guidelines might be helpful to anyone learning to write, in whatever form, for young children.

1. Know your reader and his world

Young children see everything in relation to themselves. Therefore those who write for them need to be able to think, see and feel as a child. If you can genuinely identify with a child and his world, you are well away. If not, don't despair.

Ask your friendly neighbourhood primary school for permission to observe children in the classroom, dining room and playground. Talk and listen to them. Try out your stories on them, and read them published stories. Their reactions will teach you much.

Observe children also in the park, at the swimming pool, on the beach or elsewhere. Notice or, better still, make notes on the kinds of things which make them laugh, cry, argue, and so on.

Read what they read. Ask your friendly neighbourhood librarian what books (factual as well as fictional) are popular with children of the age group in which you are interested. Spend time reading and analysing these.

Resurrect the child in yourself. This is particularly important for creative writing. Think long and hard about your own childhood. Write down your earliest memories, noting not just the external events, but your own thoughts and feelings about them. Most children love hearing stories starting, 'Once when I was five/eight/ten years old...' So try weaving your memories into impromptu stories for any children you know. These are unlikely to become, if written down, instant classics, but by story-telling, you will evoke more memories and feelings—those essential raw materials for the would-be creative writer. The main object of resurrecting the child in yourself is to enable you to identify *deeply* with a child, on the threshold of his brave new life and brave new world. Hopefully, through all these means, you will be able to open up your life again in a way that a child does, or at least to imagine what it would be like to be so receptive and unguarded; to see the world with fresh new eyes, or at least to imagine how it would look to someone seeing things in that way.

2. Write the truth but not the whole truth

Knowing your reader should lead to respecting his freedom, his emotional vulnerability, his limited experience and his developing intellect. This means that some subjects are taboo. This is not a particularly popular viewpoint these days. I once heard a woman being interviewed about a book for children which contained factual descriptions of a wide range of sexual practices including incest. Asked whether she thought children should have access to such information at all, let alone without moral guidelines, she replied, in effect, 'Children live in the real world. These things happen.' Her implication was that children should have access to any and every aspect of what *is*!

Fortunately, Christians would not stand alone in whole-heartedly opposing such a view. The world is full of cow-pats, but we do not for that reason rub the faces of newborn babies in them. The truth, for Christians anyway, must always be censored by love. Our answer to the question, 'Am I my brother's keeper?' has to be, 'Yes. Particularly if he is weak, young and vulnerable.'

On the other hand, Christian writers have tended to make *too many* subjects taboo. Quite young children these days are, unfortunately, likely to know about broken homes, bullying, vandalism and other forms of lawlessness and violence; through the media they will probably also be aware of large-scale disasters, war and want. Therefore we shouldn't avoid these topics. But the world we paint for our young readers mustn't be *too* bad or *too* sad. I would want to stop short of horror, witch-craft (stories about funny ghosts and witches, at the very least, distort reality), and the darker faces of evil and suffering. These are aspects of reality, certainly. But best postponed for as long as possible in literature. It may not, alas, be possible in life.

Early exposure to too much sin and suffering can be very damaging indeed. Christians must beware of jumping on the world's bandwagon in these matters. If, on the other hand, we feel compelled to write on a sombre theme, then we shouldn't allow the possible criticisms of fellow-Christians to deter us. After all, we do have a contribution to make, since we can offer some explanation for some of the bad or sad things that happen, and some present and future hope to anyone in sad situations.

Christian writers should also, I believe, more than balance out bad and sad realism by their portrayal of what is true, noble, right, pure, lovely, admirable, excellent and praiseworthy (Philippians 4:8). Anyone who can portray goodness as credible, dynamic and attractive would be doing something immensely worthwhile. All too often, the bad characters, or people in their pre-conversion days, come across more strongly than the 'good', converted ones. Surely we want our young readers to be drawn to what is good, to gain the impression from what we write that the world God made is a wonderful, exciting place and the life God planned a worthwhile adventure.

So out of respect for our readers vulnerable emotions and limited experience, we choose suitable themes. We must also consider his intellectual development. Generally speaking, he will not be able to grasp abstract, complex truths, so we should concentrate on what can be discovered through the senses, i.e. on the concrete and practical. In view of this, should we, I wonder, highlight for our young readers the tangible, practical dimension of our faith? Certainly, it is far easier to weave a credible tale from the *observable* apsects of Christianity that it is from these things which may only be known through *revelation*. Paul Tournier is again relevant here: 'The hand of God is not to be seen in abstract ideas, but in nature, in history, in all the adventures of men.'

3. Watch your tone

Two attitudes to be avoided, I believe, are sentimentality, and humour *at the child's expense*. We must at all costs avoid the written equivalents of using a 'twee' voice, 'talking down', patting our young reader on the head, calling him sweet and commenting on his dimples. Someone had aptly named this attitude '*hand-chubbery*', an illusion to the typically sentimental phrase, 'chubby little hands'.

Hand-chubbery is not nearly as common as it used to be, but it is not entirely extinct. Generally speaking, the older one grows and the further removed from real children one is, the easier it becomes to sentimentalise, idolise or idealise the young. So grandparents and great-uncles who want to write for this age group—beware!

On the other hand, there occasionally appears a spate of books which purport to be humorous tales for children, but are in fact encouraging the reader to laugh *at* the child. Fortunately, these usually sink without trace after enjoying a brief vogue among adults. Humour is very important, but at the child's level so that he can join in the laughter.

4. Mind your language

The words we use must, in the main, be understood by the child. I heard one writer for young children boast that he never used a short word where a long one would do. I think that is just as misguided as limiting yourself to one-syllable, plain words all the time. One picture book I opened began with this sentence: 'In a top-secret, military research establishment, set deep in the heart of Africa, a computer was restless.' Department of Utter Confusion for the average under-five, I thought!

It's right to be aware of what words your readers are likely to know and to use them. But it is also good to include a smattering of unfamiliar words to stretch or just to delight them. I remember the joy and amusement with which ours, when quite small, hailed the new word 'lullaby'. They didn't, I think, fully understand what it meant, but they chuckled over the *sound* of it for days and days, repeating it gleefully to one another.

The important thing is to choose the word that most exactly conveys what you want to say. If a short, familiar word will do that, then use it by all means. If the best word is a longer, unfamiliar one, don't hesitate to use that, either.

At all costs, let's avoid jargon, including Christian jargon. I heard a well-known speaker pray, just before his talk at an all-age family service, that God would bless the collection just received to the extension of his church in this corner of his vineyard?' Department of Utter Confusion again! Jargon presupposes too much or conveys too little or nothing. It often includes words or ideas that are woolly, euphemistic or lacking in force through overuse.

5. Know what you want to say and think deeply about it

This suggestion applies especially to creative writers. We can't say *everything*, so we need to choose what, particularly, we want to say. Woolly writing is often the result of an author's not knowing precisely what it is he wants to say. And if our writing is to be original rather than common-place, deep feelings and thoughts must be involved. Jane Gardam has said, 'I wrote my books...because I so badly wanted to write them.'

Writers need to meditate often, both in a spiritual and general sense. We need to formulate our beliefs, recognise and analyse our emotions and think deeply about our beha-viour and its causes, all this not as an end in itself, but to help us become more perceptive about people, and to make us aware of what we have to offer in the way of what may be described as raw materials and raw talents. We might need more of both, and certainly both will need to be refined by hard work and skill, before we are able to produce anything good enough for publication. Even when we do that, rejec-tions are likely to be plentiful, so a sense of call and persistence are once again necessary.

6. Get writing

Like most postscripts this is crucial. Unless you positively disagree with what you have been asked to write, you would do well to seize every opportunity that comes your way, however long or short the piece of writing may be, and whether your efforts will be noticed and paid for, or not. A job is only trivial if you tackle it in that way. Children's lives, if not those of the rest of us consist mainly of so-called trivialities. Tackle anything trivially, and your writing will be trivial. Tackle something creatively, giving it all you've got, and you may surprise yourself by producing something original and stylish. If you turn down assignments or opportunities while waiting for the big break or the great idea, you could well wait for ever. If you are faithful in what is least, you will probably be trusted with bigger projects nearer to your heart. It's likely that much poor, third-rate writing will come from our pen or typewriter, however hard we try, before any good, excellent writing appears. But if we keep writing to our top limits, and stay in touch with our readers and in tune with ourselves, we will improve. And if Jesus Christ is at the centre of all our living, thinking, and feeling, then he will be able to communicate his truth through our writing to our readers. Not all of it all the time. But some of it all of the time.

All writing, but particularly that for young children, needs to be seen 'as an adventure directed by God' (Paul Tournier).

Useful books

Edward Blishen (ed.), *The Thorny Paradise* (Writers on Writing for Children), Kestrel Books.
Margery Fisher, *Intent Upon Reading* (revised edition of her critical appraisal of modern fiction for children), Brockhampton Press.
Marjorie Boulton, *The Anatomy of Prose*, Routledge & Kegan Paul.
John Fairfax, John Moat, *The Way to Write*, Elm Tree Books.
Ivan Southall, *A Journey of Discovery*, Kestrel Books.
Paul Tournier, *The Adventure of Living*, Highland Books.

Chapter Five

WRITING FOR RADIO

By

David Winter

'The potential audience for radio is vast.'

David Winter is Head of BBC Religious Programmes Radio and the author of twelve books, including *Hereafter*, which became a bestseller and has been translated into various languages, *The Case for Christ*, *The Search for the Real Jesus* and *Living Through Loss*. He was for some years editor of *Crusade* before joining the BBC as a producer.

One of the very few expanding markets for writers is radio. As print on paper slowly and reluctantly gives way to electronic letters and figures on a screen—as it surely must, one sad, sad day—so the outlets for the written word in its spoken form will surely increase. In Britain alone, by 1986 there will be 38 BBC local radio stations forming a network over the whole of England, with two national stations for Wales (one in English, one in Welsh), another for Scotland and yet another for Northern Ireland. On present plans, these will operate alongside the existing four national Networks (Radio 1, 2, 3, and 4) and a new Network 5, backing up the local radio output.

In competition with that formidable army of transmitters there will be what amounts to a national network of independent (commercial) radio stations, probably passing the fifty mark by the late 'eighties. And twenty years ago local radio had not begun in Britain!

This tremendous explosion of radio broadcasting is paralleled by a slow but persistent decline in the number of periodical outlets for the aspiring journalist, yet relatively few people have discerned the trend and put their main efforts into writing for the media of the future (TV and radio). Certainly very few Christians would be able to lay their hands on their hearts and say that they would rather write a ten minute feature for radio, with an audience of, say, 100,000, than see their name in print at the top of an article in an established religious periodical (circulation, say 20,000). Vanity rules?

The potential audience for radio is, of course, much larger than that. Virtually every home in Britain has a radio set, usually two or three. The measured audience for the religious '*Pause for Thought*' slot on Radio 2 every weekday morning is something like four million. '*Thought for the Day*' on Radio 4 is heard by well over a million, and comparable talks on the most successful of the local BBC and ILR stations can reach as many as thirty per cent. of the entire population of an area. Imagine telling a visiting evangelist that he would have the chance to address a third of the population of Sheffield, Liverpool or Glasgow!

Even more specialised religious programmes can reach huge audiences. Gerald Priestland's investigative series on Christian doctrine, '*Priestland's Progress*', drew a regular late Sunday night audience on Radio 4 approaching half a million—and a postbag, by the end of the 13-week series, of over 24,000 letters. With its mid-week repeat it was probably heard by nearly a million people a week—more than twice the number who watch League football. And after that, the book of the series was on the bestsellers list for most of 1982!

I am saying all this because I am aware that many would-be Christian writers simply do not think of radio as a possible outlet for their work. This can be for many reasons other than the vanity which I rather unkindly attributed to them. Some may feel that competition is too intense, or that radio is a 'closed shop' to a small coterie of distinguished experts. Some may hesitate to embark on an unfamiliar sea. Some may have tried, and been rebuffed. And some may feel that there is a special mystique about writing for radio which they do not have, and do not know how they can acquire.

This chapter is for all such people. Radio is not a closed shop. There is no exclusive coterie of radio writers. Competition is strong, but no stronger than in the periodical or book field, and less so than in national newspapers. And while there is a technique, or rather a number of techniques, there is no mystique to radio writing.

The medium

Radio is a spoken medium. If that sounds obvious, I can only give it as my experience over many years that the biggest flaw in radio script writing is that people treat radio as if it were made of paper. There is an enormous difference between the way we express ourselves in print, and the way we speak. I do not mean the difference between conversational and written English, but the difference between spoken English, even of a fairly formal kind (such as a sermon) and written English. The first step in writing for radio is to establish in our minds right from the start that these are words to be *heard*, not read. The crucial test of a piece of writing for radio is to read it out aloud.

The second thing about radio as a medium is that it depends upon just one sense: sound. Basically, it is life with a blindfold on! The radio writer may well create in the listener's imagination visual images, tactile sensations, even smells. But they will all enter through the same gate: the ear. Again, that may sound obvious. And again I can only give it as my experience that many, many people forget it, or have never really grasped it. Consequently they end up writing television without pictures; one of the most common complaints of script editors about the submissions of would-be radio dramatists as well. The good radio writer turns this apparent disadvantage—the single, sense nature of the medium—to his advantage, evoking sights, feels and smells that the seeming realism of television or the stage cannot reproduce. As one distinguished critic said, plays are always better on the radio because the pictures are better. He might have added that the characters always look the way we imagined them when we read the book!

Radio is not just a powerful evoker of images, however. It is also a splendid medium for ideas and argument. A book or article has the advantage that you can go back and re-read a difficult paragraph, but radio has the priceless asset of shutting the mind in to the words, not just as shapes on the paper, but as sounds expressing all those nuances of inflection, tone of voice and emphasis that make speech the definitive means of communication between human beings. What we would give, for instance, for a recording of the Sermon on the Mount, to settle all the arguments about whether such-and-such was ironical, or hyperbole, or sternly spoken, or with the tongue in the cheek!

I believe that is why radio is so effective as a medium of debate, and why those who argue their case on the radio, whether it be political, religious or artistic, invariably get a greater response than when they do the same thing on television or in print. The volume of correspondence to the religious broadcasting department of BBC radio is far greater than to our colleagues in television. In fact, broadcasters are frequently astonished that a broadcast talk or sermon can evoke, on occasions, literally thousands of letters. Frank Topping, who writes and broadcasts a weekly meditation on '*Pause for Thought*' on Radio 2, has a postbag that runs into thousands of letters a month, most of them responding to specific things that he has said.

The third great factor about radio as a medium is that it is one-to-one. Although the speaker may well be addressing thousands or millions of people, woe betide him if he forgets that he is addressing each one as an individual listener. Radio, especially in its modern usage, is a highly personal medium, usually listened to by one person on his own, or at the most by two or three people, for instance, in a car together. Radio is the companion of our lonely hours. It talks to the young mother alone at home with her toddler. It accompanies the commercial traveller along the motorways on his business travels. It is fed into the ear of the teenager with his 'Walkman' wherever he goes. And through the night's long watches its words and music keep company with the old, the sleepless and the shift worker. The voice from the radio should be the voice of a friend, or at any rate of an invited guest, ushered into the most intimate locations of our lives. In the circumstances in which radio is used nowadays, it is simply folly to use it as a megaphone to address a crowd. It is, often literally, the voice at our elbow.

The principles

The principles of writing for radio are pretty well the same for every kind of programme. Indeed, many of them flow from the kind of things I have been saying about the nature of the medium.

The first and most basic is to remember that radio is a speech medium. This means that simple, direct English is infinitely more effective than the formal style, with longer sentences and subordinate clauses, that we associate with writing.

Let me give you an example. The following passage might well appear as an editorial in a Christian magazine:

> What should our attitude be towards those Christians from whom we differ? That is a question raised by such events as *"The Week of Prayer for Christian Unity"*. As we meet with fellow-Christians from different traditions, holding different beliefs—people from whom we prefer to remain separated throughout the rest of the year—we are challenged afresh to face the words of Christ. He prayed that his followers might be 'perfectly one', *so that the world might believe*. The embarrassing truth is that we have not even been imperfectly one; and the world has not believed.

Now let us suppose that a speaker on the radio wanted to make much the same point. I think a good script might put it like this:

> This is *"The Week of Prayer for Christian Unity"*. Every time it comes round I feel a bit embarrassed. You see, for fifty-one weeks of the year, if I'm absolutely honest, I'm quite happy to

pray along with those who agree with me, with "my" church. I actually prefer my separated brethren to stay separated. But then, once a year, regular as clockwork, there comes the reminder of what Jesus said. He prayed that his followers would be "perfectly one". And we're not. And he said that if we *were*, the "world would believe". And it doesn't.

The difference between the two pieces is not a difference of quality, but of approach. The first is intended to be read. The second is intended to be spoken. In the spoken version there are no subordinate clauses apart from parentheses. The thing moves along quickly, and phrases like 'you see', which are both unnecessary and ugly in written English, help to create a feeling of intimacy and naturalness.

The other important difference is that the radio piece is in the first person. The listener hears a *voice*, and a voice is a manifestation of personality. That is why the first person works so well on the radio, and often less well in print. Radio is the medium of personal experience, shared in an apparently intimate broadcaster-to-listener context.

Writing for radio best suits those who express themselves in sharp, concise, forceful and memorable terms. It is not the ideal place for a measured, linear argument (though it is better for this than television), but it *is* a medium where words and phrases stick. I am often astonished at how accurately people can recall things said on the radio, often verbatim, though they have only heard them once, and fleetingly. Radio repays the writer who takes the trouble to write a powerful compact topic sentence, or can sum up his case in a short, arresting phrase. And radio also permits and indeed rewards the writer who is not afraid to repeat himself, if necessary over and over again, though not always in the same words. This follows from the point I made earlier. It is possible to go back and re-read a difficult or demanding paragraph in a book. Radio (apart from the growing use of cassette recordings) only offers one chance to hear the words. Then they are gone, usually for ever.

67

The practice

From those general principles we can move on to consider the different kinds of programmes on the radio. We shall ignore those that do not concern the writer: that increasingly long list of unscripted and often unplanned phone-ins, record shows, chat shows and round-the-table discussions. The remaining output can be broken down into news bulletins, talks, features and documentaries, drama and light entertainment.

News bulletins are, of course, a specialist sphere, but many local radio stations now carry a bulletin of local and national religious news, often written by a freelance contributor. My own first contribution to radio was just such a bulletin, and writing it week after week was an excellent crash course in writing for radio! I had to shed the journalistic habits of a lifetime, and go for short, clear sentences, with many more conjunctions and many fewer prepositions than I had been accustomed to use. As I had to read it on air myself, I quickly learnt to avoid phrases which were virtually unreadable. Try reading aloud, 'The suffragan bishop of the diocese of St. Edmundsbury and Ipswich'!

A good news bulletin, I have learnt subsequently, is a work of art. The selection of the items and of the order in which they appear, the clarity of the language and the essential accuracy both of fact and impression given, these qualities are not easily or quickly acquired. Most people can recognise a bad bulletin when they hear one, but a good bulletin should pass unnoticed. The great art is to conceal art!

Talks are the normal 'nursery slope' for new broadcasters. On most stations there is some spot, often daily, for Christian reflection; and most stations find it hard to find enough people to do it even competently, let alone well. That is why you tend to hear the same men and women over and over again on programmes like '*Thought for the Day*'. They are the tried and trusted contributors, battle-hardened, if you like.

There is great rejoicing in the production offices when another name can be added to their ranks. Up and down the country, of course, there must be literally hundreds of people who contribute fairly regularly to some such spot. A few are brilliant, some are excellent occasionally, and always competent. Some are usually dreadful, and just occasionally competent. May I say that very seldom if ever is the determining factor theology. It is nearly always a misuse or abuse of the medium, producing a strong, negative reaction in the listener.

The most common misuse of the medium by Christians is to regard the radio talk as a sermon or a talk to a church gathering. As we have seen, radio is an intimate, one-to-one medium, so it is patently wrong to write a radio talk that addresses people in the mass. A radio talk should never include anything that you could not say to the listener if you were chatting to him as a guest in his sitting room. That is a pretty accurate rule of thumb.

The other major misuse of the radio talk is to try to get too many points into it. Ideally, a talk of five minutes or less should aim to say *one* thing, to say it clearly, memorably and frequently. When you have written your talk, read it to yourself aloud. That is quite simply the acid test.

Feature and documentary writing are more ambitious. Most radio stations mount the occasional documentary programme, and they are very common on Radio 4 and Radio 3. Some of these documentaries are made up almost entirely of pre-recorded interviews and actuality, with only the minimum of scripted material, usually written by the presenter. But many are basically illustrated essays, depending from first to last on good research and high quality writing. If you are interested in writing for radio documentary or feature programmes, the first qualification is to listen to them, not just one or two, but every one you can possibly catch for a month or two. In that way you will absorb the form and texture of them and, I guess, begin to respect them as a genuine if transitory art form.

It may be possible then to do some freelance work as a researcher on such a programme, which would provide further 'on the job' experience, involving some writing skills as well as pure research.

Having familiarised yourself with the medium, you may now feel in a position to put up an idea for a documentary programme, or series of programmes. Usually you will choose a subject on which you already have some expertise, or at least in which you have a keen interest. Do not be too ambitious. Series on 'The History of the Jewish People' or 'A Christian Approach to the Problems of the Inner City' are not likely to be accepted from a first-time caller (to use the jargon of the 'phone-in). First establish a track record, then go for the mega-subjects.

So, instead of those panoramic subjects, narrow things down: 'The Diary of an East End Jew', perhaps, or 'The Crypt of St Martin's'. Set your proposal out on a single sheet of paper, under a few headings: the aim and scope of the programme, the method to be used (on-site interviews, dramatised readings, book extracts, music, and so on), and your own role in it (researcher/writer, perhaps, or deviser and writer). Make it clear whether or not you see yourself as the programme's presenter.

Then send your proposal to a producer. If you have been listening to programmes, you will have heard, or read in the *Radio Times*, the names of people who produce the kind of programmes you are interested in doing. Do not expect instant success (though it does come, from time to time), but accept any invitation to take the matter further, talk it over or adapt your idea into an existing series.

If your idea is accepted, you will work very closely with the producer, and provided you really *can* write, and have some ear for radio, you should not have too many problems. Making a documentary is a bit like making a case in court. It is your case, but you need to introduce your witnesses. The only difference is that on the radio you have to bring in the witnesses for both sides, and be fair to both, whatever your personal views or beliefs may be. That is the nature of a documentary, at any rate in Britain.

Radio drama is a separate subject in itself, but I cannot omit it because it is both the most demanding and also the best rewarded writing on the radio. It is also an area where the Christian dramatist can make a powerful contribution.

Again, the first qualifications is to listen to radio drama, hours and hours of it. Some of the very finest dramatists of our time write radio drama. Tom Stoppard's latest play was written specifically for BBC radio. So it is not a painful duty to immerse oneself in it. It is a medium that rewards the wordsmith; the dramatist whose principle talent is dialogue. But it also provides scope for those who want to use an enormous canvas. The sets are free! Radio drama can roam through time and space, can create magic and illusion, can people heaven and earth with characters. It requires imagination, and a profound working knowledge of the medium, but it is worthwhile.

Much the same applies to radio light entertainment. Because television pays better, radio has become the training ground for the up and coming generation of comedy writers. It is voracious for talent, and those who can be genuinely funny and convey that humour through a radio script, will find that they are eagerly taken up and encouraged.

In the case of both drama and light entertainment, most of the opportunities of writing for radio are within the BBC, though some of the larger ILR stations have presented excellent, original drama. Drama scripts and ideas should be sent to the Radio Scripts Editor, Drama Department. Light entertainment (comedy) scripts to the Radio Scripts Editor, or the producer of a specified programme. And both addresses are at BBC, Broadcasting House, London W1A 1AA. Those who would like to try their hand at a straight story to be read aloud on the radio, should send scripts (about 2,200 words) to the Editor, 'Morning Story', at the same address or to their Regional Network address. Again, be sure to listen to the programme many times before you set pen to paper. It is *not* wasted time.

Writing for radio will not make you a millionaire, though it is not badly paid: from a minimum of about £60 for that 'Morning Story' up to a four-figure sum for the average full-length radio drama. Local radio fees are much smaller, of course, and some do not pay at all for short talks. But for those who have something to say, and a burning desire to say it, the radio provides an ideal platform.

Forty years ago C. S. Lewis used the radio for his famous '*Broadcast Talks*', which brought before a war-torn and battered people the vision of a wider truth. Religious broadcasting today is looking for a modern C. S. Lewis. Until you try you cannot be sure that you are not the person.

1. A useful reference book is: *Writing for the BBC* 7th Edition. 1983. Price £1.75.
   Available from booksellers. Or write direct to: BBC, 35 Marylebone High Street, London W1M 4AA.
   This book includes the Regional Network addresses.
2. A passage of typical radio documentary script is illustrated below. It was taken from a programme about the Pope's 1982 visit to Great Britain.

TAPE: *IN*   On this first visit…
         OUT: …..as one who serves   1.14″

There were ceremonial embraces between the leaders of the churches; Roman and Anglican, Orthodox and Pentecostal and Free Church. The kisses on either cheek were formal; but Pope John Paul's handshakes were vigorous and long. The central moment—the proof of common faith and good faith—was when Archbishop, Pope and Free Church Moderator together invited all to renew the vows of baptism…

TAPE: *IN:*   Do you turn…..
         OUT: …son and Holy Spirit.   1.48″

Christianity has long been a divided faith; but in each church men and women have died for the same basic belief; and movingly, the martyrs of our own time were remembered.

Their deaths are raw and ugly, unromanticized by centuries of history; candles were lit for Martin Luther King; for Archbishop Luwum of Uganda; for Cardinal Romero of El Salvador and for Father Kolbe, the Polish priest who died in Auschwitz. The people sang for them, and for all the unsung saints and heroes of our own time...

TAPE: *FOR ALL THE SAINTS*   (*Fade*, end of v.1)   0.56"

So many old taboos and precedents were broken today in Canterbury Cathedral that a minor one—the fact that unrestrained, un-Anglican applause broke out when the Pope came in—might well pass unremarked. Afterwards, a decorous assembly of churchmen, in purple and red, and black robes and beard for the orthodox Archbishop of Thyateria—surrounded the figure of the Pope in his simple white, and there were more handshakes and presentations and smiles, in the Deanery Garden.

At Wembley, however, the crowds were massing in what Cardinal Hume described as one enormous parish church— waiting on the Cup Final turf, and preparing a less decorous welcome...

TAPE   *FX CLAPPING AND SINGING*   0.29

Chapter Six

WRITING IN PARTNERSHIP

By

David Phypers

'Two heads are better than one.'

So far all of David Phypers' books have been written jointly with Donald Bridge. It has been a remarkable partnership. Their first title published by IVP *Spiritual Gifts and the Church* sold almost 50,000 copies. Most of their books have been published in America and some have been translated.

David, an Anglican, is a schoolmaster, and Donald is the minister of Frinton Free Church, Frinton-on-Sea. Their last book, published by Hodder and Stoughton, is *Growing in God's Family*.

'Two heads are better than one.' This is why Don Bridge and I have kept on writing books together for the past ten years. We improve each other's work. All of us have strengths and weaknesses, blind spots and areas of understanding and perception. Writing is lonely work. You can agonise over a script, write it and re-write it, only to have it rejected by a publisher or ripped up by a reviewer. But if you have someone with whom to share the load, someone to compensate for your shortcomings, to complement your ability, then you are fortunate indeed.

When you write in tandem with someone else, you have an immediate critic of your work. You need one. Of course, you will criticise your work yourself. You will read it, correct it, improve the odd turn of phrase here and there, but you will only criticise it within your own terms of reference. Someone else will see faults in your argument and your presentation that you will never notice. If you are not corrected before you publish, you certainly will be afterwards.

Don and I are ruthless in our criticism of each other. Everyone has a bad day sometimes, a bad week, a bad month. When one of us writes badly, the other one tells us in no uncertain terms. When we write well we are equally fulsome in our praise.

In my youth I enjoyed the benefit of a university education. For years I learned to write academic essays, to organise my material, to present it in a logical and orderly fashion, to give due weight to varied opinions, to avoid red herrings, to acknowledge sources and to draw valid conclusions. So when I started writing books, I simply carried on writing university essays! They were sound, worthy and dull.

Don's 'university' was Hyde Park Corner, Liverpool Pier Head and every racecourse in Britain. In eight years with the Open Air Mission he learned to catch people's attention with a topical story, to hold it with colourful illustrations and to present the gospel in language that everyone could understand. His mentors were the *Daily Mirror* and the *Daily Express* with their ability to express ideas succinctly in five-word sentences and two-syllable words. When he started writing he brought colour, vitality and immediacy to his work in sharp contrast to my prosaic style.

But Don did not always know when to stop. In his excitement and enthusiasm for his subject he would sometimes get carried away from the subject on which he was supposed to be writing. Or he would illustrate a point with a super story which did not really illustrate the point at all!

Together, we make a good team. My academic training enables me to lay a book out and to plan the course of a chapter. Don sparks up our work, hooks the browser and keeps him hooked when I might send him to sleep!

When you write together you enjoy the benefit of your combined knowledge. We both read widely, Don more so than I. We have particular areas of Christian history and understanding in which we have a special interest. Sometimes our interests are the same, sometimes they are different. Either way we benefit. Together we must have saved each other hours in research when we have brought our separate understanding together into the books we have written.

Through writing together we have saved each other from extreme opinions and overstated conclusions. These are the common pitfalls of every author. Some publishers pander to anything controversial. In our books we have often written about sensitive issues on which Christians hold strong opinions. It would have been so easy to have ground our personal axes, to have deepened the divisions between Christians rather than to have healed them. More than once we have said to each other, 'I could not put my name to that.' And so we have restrained each other and saved ourselves from folly.

Getting started

If you are going to write successfully with someone else you must both enjoy a deep, mutual trust in each other. Don and I became firm friends during six years when we were pastor and deacon respectively in the same church. That friendship has never wavered since, though at times, through our writing, it has been tested to breaking-point. Only because of our shared respect have we come back from the brink on these occasions.

If either of you is jealous of the other, if you suspect the other's motives, if you try and steal a march on the other in what you write or in the way you criticise his or her work, you will come to grief. You must be totally honest with each other, and willing to recognise that when your partner disagrees with you he does so from the very best of motives.

Then you must share the same basic convictions in your understanding of the Christian faith. It is not enough both to be Christians. You must know where you stand with respect to the Bible, the nature of the gospel and the mission of the church to the world. If you differ fundamentally in these areas you will lack the commonality of purpose which will give your work distinctive force and direction.

Our faith is deeply rooted in the Reformed and Evangelical traditions. We believe the gospel is about forgiveness and spiritual regeneration. The church's mission is primarily spiritual rather than social. Our areas of agreement are wide yet again and again we have fought each other to a standstill on one point or another. When we were writing *Growing in God's Family* we were surprised to find we differed quite sharply on the nature of Christian holiness. Eventually, we found a way through because our basic convictions were the same. Had they not been, we would have failed. As it was, that experience made us wonder if, perhaps, our writing partnership should end. After years in which our thinking had moved along similar lines, was it now diverging to the point where joint writing would become dishonest?

A further qualification for joint authorship is a common desire to communicate through the printed word. Don is primarily a preacher, and a fine one at that. If he ever thought about writing he never found the time, until I enthused him with the idea of *Spiritual Gifts and the Church*. Writing is both exciting and depressing. Few authors get it right first time. It is very time consuming. You can write a good book and see it fail in sales terms. Your work will be scorned by supercilious reviewers. Unless you both believe in the power of the printed word, unless you both share the urge to see your work in print, there is no point in writing together.

Then, of course, if you are going to write together, you must be willing to compromise. For all sorts of reasons, precisely what you want to say will not find its way on to the printed page. But you will agree to compromise because you will realise that what you eventually agree together is better than what either of you would have written on your own. 'Two heads are better than one.'

Doing the job

How you write together will vary according to who you are and the nature of your different strengths. Far more books are jointly produced than is always obvious from the author's name on the cover. One of the greatest preachers of the twentieth century, whose sermons were published and are still read by thousands, thought that his words simply needed to be turned into print to produce instant bestsellers. His daughter knew better. She carefully edited all his work, removed the frequent repetitions (which passed unnoticed in the pulpit but would have jarred in print) and generally tidied up his material for publication. All of Martyn Lloyd-Jones' books were, in fact, the fruit of joint authorship.

Turning sermons into books is one very good way of writing together—if your minister knows how to preach! Our first book arose out of some of Don's sermons on the Holy Spirit with additional material of my own. We have discussed repeating the procedure with other series at some time in the future.

Writing together does not necessarily mean you both have to put words on paper. Many books are 'ghosted'. Someone tells you a story, on tape perhaps, and you write it up. (*Chasing the Dragon*, by Jackie Pullinger, was largely written by Andrew Quicke.) Usually one name goes on the cover. You might not be acknowledged at all, or maybe you might receive an insignificant mention. Or you might write for a partner who does the research and feeds you with the material. A former *Daily Express* journalist used to turn out 100,000 word bestsellers in this way. His partner perhaps spent five months in Japan; the journalist wrote up the result.

We have found that one of us must be architect, though both may build. Usually, but not always, I have conceived and planned the structure of the books and then we have both put material into them. John and Elizabeth Sherrill work in a similar way. He builds the house, she furnishes it and puts the clouds in the sky!

Once we start writing we often plan in advance to write particular chapters, but we still send all our work to each other, review it, alter it and sometimes rewrite it completely. On occasions a chapter will go backwards and forwards several times with each of us making further alterations each time, until we are sure we have got it right. This makes it all the more amusing when reviewers try 'higher criticism' of our work, defining who has written what. They are invariably wrong!

When we started writing we lived within a mile of each other and could easily meet to discuss the way the book was going. Now that we live nearly two hundred miles apart that kind of regular contact is impossible. So sometimes we use the 'phone (expensive), and very occasionally we have met in London for a day for extended discussion. Even more occasionally we have taken some holiday in each other's home and found time for discussion then.

As we write I am constantly editing, moulding the combined material into what I hope will be the finished product, ready for the publisher. When I was sixteen my father gave me an old typewriter and a half-crown booklet, *Typewriting Self-Taught*. Learning to type was one of the best things I ever did. It has saved us hours of work and the expense of employing a typist to present our work in acceptable form.

Footnotes are a constant headache. If you quote from another writer you must acknowledge his name, book or article, page number, publisher and date of edition in a footnote. Such a diversion obviously hinders your writing flow, yet the only way I have found to keep on top of the problem and not to lose this precise information, is to write the footnotes as I go along. I put the footnotes to one page at the top of the next page and in this way keep them close to the material to which they refer. They are a chore, but vital if your work is to have that professional touch to commend it to publisher and readers alike.

Finally, your work is done, or you think it is. You read through the typescript for the last time, correct any remaining errors, check the quotations and footnotes, see that all the pages are in the correct order and send it off. When we had finished *Growing in God's Family* our publisher kindly lent us an office for the day. We sat together, went through the script page by page, altered it, argued over it, improved it and finally left it behind for editing and publishing. Surprisingly, we had never carried out such a final joint exercise before; we wished we had.

Difficulties

Quite apart from the personal disagreements which may arise, joint authorship also presents its own particular problems. Not the least of these is time. Unless you have private means and can therefore afford to write whenever you wish, or unless you write an instant bestseller and can live off the profits, finding time to write will always be a problem. In that, Don and I are no different from anyone else. Most of my writing is done in the evenings, after wearing days in the classroom. Sometimes I escape into a caravan in the garden and write there. Don fits his writing into the heavy demands of leading a large and growing church.

But writing together compounds the problem of time. One of you may have time, while the other may not. One of you may have the urge to write and so make time, while the other may feel that something else is more important. If you are writing different chapters you may feel you cannot continue until your partner has contributed the next instalment. So you end up badgering and waiting impatiently.

When we started writing we had no idea that, if you want to write a book, you should prepare a synopsis, write a specimen chapter, and tempt a publisher (or an agent) with the goodies you have on offer. The last thing you should do is to send a completed manuscript without warning to a publisher, hoping he will find it the scoop of the century and make you famous overnight! But that is exactly what we did, and with a pretty rotten script to boot.

Nevertheless, being green had its advantages. Because we finished our work first (or thought we did), we were spared the problem of working to a publisher's deadline. We could at least work at our own pace without the fear that if we failed to finish by a certain date we would lose a contract.

Later, writing to such deadlines proved an enormous headache. When we signed the contract for a deadline several months away we seemed to have plenty of time. Then the problems began. Although we knew what we wanted to write we somehow could not get going. Inspiration dried up. All kinds of petty commitments got in the way. Don came home from Israel with a virus infection which drained his energy and sapped his creativity. Unless you know you are going to have plenty of time to write, beware of signing a contract for an unwritten or unfinished book if you are going to write together.

Style is another problem with joint authorship. When you write solo you obviously write in your own distinctive style which, hopefully, attracts a readership which will eventually read your stuff just because you have written it. But when you write together, particularly if you both contribute, creating a unified style is much more difficult. Perhaps because we both edit each other's work and I carry out a final editing of our joint effort we have overcome the problem to a degree, but it still remains.

A further problem is finance. When you sign your contract with your publisher he will probably offer you between seven-and-a-half and ten per cent of the retail price as royalties. But when there are two of you, you only count as one for royalties' purposes. So you only receive half of what you would have if you write alone. Only a few Christian writers ever make enough money to live on from their writing. If you write together that livelihood is halved.

Rewards

If the financial reward for joint authorship is small it is far outweighed by others. Researching and writing about sensitive areas of Christian understanding has been reward in itself. Listening to each other, exploring seeming contradictions which often prove to be complementary, breaking out of the verbalisms which make for trench-warfare rather than Christian reconciliation has been a deeply humbling experience. We have had to stop using odd texts (often out of context) as theological hand-grenades, and help each other to see and hear what the whole movement of Scripture is saying. We are the richer for it.

Then come those moments when somebody admits to reading one of your books, actually enjoying it and finding it helpful. Piously, you can give all the glory to God, but on a human level you have to share that praise with someone else, and that too keeps you from becoming proud. We recommend joint authorship, for all its drawbacks, and hope others will follow in our footsteps.

Chapter Seven

WRITING FOR
THE NATIONAL PRESS

By

Martyn Halsall

'He had better come with integrity.'

Martyn Halsall is the Churches Correspondent of *The Guardian*. He has been a journalist for 12 years, starting on local and regional newspapers, and joining *The Guardian* staff four years ago.

The week in Westminster was almost over. The members, having received their final blessing, were shuffling their order papers together and talking of train times and homo-sexuality. The second subject had been discussed formally for most of the morning. Members appeared to think it was not now quite as bad as it used to be. Another meeting of the General Synod of the Church of England had just ended. For the Press one man had provided the story of the week; a clergyman who had both confessed his own homosexuality, for the first time in public, and told of how each morning he prayed to be freed from it. As the last journalists were packing their bags in the Press room a rare visitor arrived from the tabloid end of Fleet Street. A photographer slouched in afterwards. 'Where's this gay vicar, then?' he demanded.

The churches and the Press are not exactly overwhelmed by each other's importance or integrity. Many a Christian still sees the Press as sensationalist and uninformed in its dealings with the churches. Many a newspaper will still only turn its attention to ecclesiastical affairs when scandal or eccentricity wears a dog-collar. The 'typical journalist' is still seen, in the view from the pew, as only too often interested in all the wrong things. But he cannot always be blamed if his image of churches remains dominated by buildings and dog collars. For it is too rarely an image the churches are eager to dispel.

In an age which prides itself on advanced communication the gap between pew and print remains a wide one. Only two of the national daily newspapers, the *Times* and the *Guardian*, have full-time, religious affairs correspondents. Only three of the major churches, The Church of England, Roman Catholic and Methodist churches, have full-time Press Officers. The British Council of Churches, which has some twenty-seven denominations among its members, has no full-time Press officer. This is partly because the churches themselves do not regard the post as sufficiently important to fund it.

This strange concoction of suspicion and silence conditions the role of any Christian sensing a vocation towards the media. He had better come with integrity, for any journalist quickly sniffs out the charlatan and the propogandist. He had better be informed and wise, for restrictions of time and space are the albatross round every journalist's neck. He had better be prepared, for there is no room in hard, professional journalism for the clumsy amateur. But he and she had better come. They had better make the first move, for the newspaper world is not a place of gentle presences and widely opened doors, so much as a world of tight corners where a space has to be bargained for.

It is also a place of rules and of hard-won integrity. Before Christians consider their burning mission to reform the newspaper industry, they had better think carefully just what they want to do; how and to whom. They might play God's PR to the spiritual weeklies and even attempt that role with local Press in their own town. But they are unlikely to succeed unless the ground rules are known, appreciated and adhered to. And for too long the churches have been the wide-eyed apostles of incomprehension in a cynical world.

But if they are undeterred by conventional difficulties, the impersonal becomes personal. You decide to take on the challenge. You will need a market and a role, and the best place to start is at home. Unless you are a member of a professional association, the National Union of Journalists or the Institute of Journalists, you must bear in mind the possibility of taking over someone else's legitimate work. There are still newspapers willing to accept amateur contributions, and print them as submitted, but it is not a practise leading to a better, or a freer, Press. Essentially the role of the non-professional journalist who liases with the newspaper world must be accepted as that of an adviser.

At its very broadest and most basic this involves telling a local newspaper what your church is doing. The market for this on local newspapers is usually enthusiastic, not to say voracious at quiet times of the year, but not always the most satisfactory. At its worst it confounds the popular myths of empty buildings and musty hassocks. Frequently it says only that the church is socially alive and spiritually captivated by flower festivals and drama club thrillers. The subject is immense and needs some reasonable handling.

In all cases the password is contact. A church preparing to tell of itself to the world needs self-knowledge and expertise. A Press officer needs to be appointed; not just an overworked clergyman but someone with a feel for the work. Journalists are created partly by intuition, partly by training; never conscripted. To be a good journalist is as much a gift as a concert pianist or an imaginative artist. This is not the revelation it might appear. It is just that the majority of churches have yet to make that adjustment in their theology of creation. The Press officer will be marinated in fascination for newspapers; quick to spot the 'good story'; knowing when to leave the rubbish alone. A natural curiosity will be grafted on to tact; an easy accessibility to an organised mind and a way with words.

The Press officer will need to liase with the church leadership, and the Christian community at every level. A full list of organisations and their members will have to be assembled, with the imperative of both home and business telephone numbers for at least two people in each organisation. Arrangements will need to be made about how and when news is to be collected. For this the Press officer will have done his homework, knowing when the local newspaper appears and its needs for when, and how, news is to be supplied.

Armed with his list, and the prior knowledge that his time and effort are not being wasted; the Press officer will arrange to meet the necessary journalist. The initial point of contact for any news organisation is always the news desk, where the flow of stories is arranged and monitored. Many local newspapers also have journalists covering a particular district or perhaps compiling a column of church news. These are now the people with whom to discuss regular contact and the presentation of information. Usually the guidelines will include only advance events, (old news is dead), typed details with names and numbers for further contact and ideas for events which might warrant a photograph or a longer report and how these might be arranged.

There will be additional opportunities and this is where the Press officer as adviser comes completely into his own. Newspapers at all levels are glad of experts, to whom they can turn for reliable advice. The Press officer will need to know his congregation, the interests of his clergy or lay pastor; the hobbies and expertise available in that Christian community he is translating to the world. When G. K. Chesterton said nothing was real unless it was local he might have been speaking on behalf of the observant local church Press officer.

Happy that person who had a former Far Eastern Broadcasting Association employee in his church when there was a coup in the Seychelles, where his contact had worked. Happy the layman who can put a local newspaper journalist in touch with his priest to comment from first hand missionary experience on the scene of a political upheaval, disaster or scandal. Happy the local paper contact who can again supply someone who was on the spot of some national news event, even far from home. Every news editor dreams of the 'good local angle'; the contact between his readership and the news story dominating Fleet Street. And then the door is wide open for not only the local, but also the local Christian interpretation and comment.

All the newspaper world loves a good writer. Many local papers offer a verbal pulpit. If there is not one then the Press officers, (who will also hopefully work together in the interests of ecumenical news gathering), should suggest one, liasing with their clergy. They should also suggest that any Christian comments should not be clergy-dominated. They may well be needed to work with those writers who are more at home with an academic essay than the sharpened 400 word thought for the week. Such comments are always the more acceptable when there is an inherent news story. It is then the Christian practice, rather than cold theology, which comes to the page, and lifts off into the reader's mind.

So the Press officer needs always to read first, think out the implications and to react quickly. When an item of news occurs he should know instinctively whether this is a single paragraph, half a column, or a feature for his local newspaper. Often he will over-react; sometimes the single paragraph will become something larger as the newspaper sees other implications, or is simply short of material. He needs to temper his amateur pride and develop his ability with humility; to be calm when he is proved wrong or when tensions arise in the church community he is reflecting.

Running parallel, but rarely meeting, is the world of the official church press. The major denominations have their weekly newspapers, of varying journalistic merit. Their staffs are often small, necessarily dedicated and frequently constrained by a conservative readership and economic instability. Their work is to reflect one denomination, although their contents are becoming increasingly ecumenical. Mostly they would welcome amateur assistance, although contact needs to be made well in advance to check their necessarily early deadlines. They would also appreciate good quality photographs and are more likely to use news items having recently taken place than the secular Press. An initial contact should be made to their news desks, with a brief letter explaining how you could help and requesting their needs and interests.

The major battle, of those for and against Christian involvement in 'dirty' areas like the Press and the arts, has been won in many places, but delaying skirmishes continue and there are still those awaiting the result, or preparing for counter-revolution. Many of us who are Christians involved in mass communication can remember being taken aside at the beginning of our careers and being warned off. The work is not everyone's vocation and there are still minefields threatening the novice and the advanced practitioner. Retreating inside a safe devotional paperback; limiting Christian participation to the merely censorious will solve nothing. The sad fact remains that Christians involved in mass media at any level will face the most criticism and the least practical help, or prayer, from their fellow-churchgoers.

Besides his contact book the Press officer will need to keep his diary and his file. His diary will look ahead to church occasions, interesting visitors, anniversaries, trips and activities by organisations, all the human milestones in the life of the church. The cuttings will record inclusions in print: a little modest display of flags and of pointers to the future. They will also underline current opportunities.

It is one of the great, but often ignored truisms of journalism, that people love reading about people. So the church is fifty years old? There could be a few paragraphs in the local paper about the history and development of a building. But what about the lady who remembers the laying of the foundation stone? That photograph she can dig out; that old order of service; those memories of the town at that time; that young minister or priest, now in retirement, but on the telephone with his own memories—suddenly those flat paragraphs become live quotes; a display of photographs is possible; some correspondence arrives for the letters' page; the story is fully alive and running.

A good Press officer would have forseen this possibility.

He would have spoken with his priest, dipped into the church archives, obtained the interest of the local newspaper and made the arrangements for a reporter to conduct an interview and the photographer to call just after the subject had been to the hairdresser's and well in time for the date of the anniversary. He would also have been realistic enough to hear the reply down the telephone on a busy week, with a by-election pending, a rate rise under debate, a major fire and a local girl emigrating to Hollywood stardom. 'Sorry, we just don't have room, apart from a few paragraphs.'

He will also know the times and seasons. A story which will be squeezed out in the busy spring and mid-autumn news periods will be welcomed with open pages just after Christmas or in the middle of the summer holidays. With good liason the local Press officer will be alert to this and be dipping into the forward plans drafted in the front of his cuttings file when an anxious reporter rings, 'just in case there's anything doing'.

To move from the local to the regional Press is to transfer from parish to diocesan level. The larger unit takes precendence; the local instance looks further away. Many of the churches will have Press liason established, dealing with regional and national newspapers. The Church of England and Roman Catholic churches usually employ priests, often working on media relations part-time with parish duties. They are often men with professional newspaper or broadcasting experience; keeping up to date with current developments through courses and in regular contact with professional journalists.

This does not deny one of the foundations of successful journalism; the need for wide and accurate sources. They will welcome help and the right sort of information. This will be the basis of a story they can pass on to newspapers with large, if not national, circulations. News judgement is the beginning of wisdom. All journalists have been contacted by someone we have known hoping we can 'squeeze something in', not on merit but on personal association. This can never be a criteria for news values. The original, the different, the radical change, the development with large-scale consequences; these are the matters to interest the regional Press. A telephone tip to the diocesan or district Press contact should be enough to register initial interest. After the provision of a few details the professional link will be made. Success can guarantee a regular inclusion in items like diocesan news sheets, although far more important is to stress individual items of interest rather than swamp a newspaper with several items from the same church source.

The Press officer should always be involved in his church magazine. If there is not one established he should develop one, however simple. There is the classic cautionary tale of the vicar who went round churches collecting large piles of parish magazines. These he consigned to a bonfire, to prevent them doing any further harm. A massive Christian restoration project needs to be established for church magazines and many useful training courses are being developed. There is much that can be done to make more professional the most humbly produced effort. And when they are likely to form an important contact with local Press this professionalism is all the more important.

For the provincial Press the ground rules for local press contact obviously still apply. Where the matter is technical or theological, imagination is essential. In post-Christian Britain there is fear of church stories among some journalists, anxious to avoid misleading information, uncertain whether the dog-collar in front of them is Mr. or Father, dubious of what terms and ground rules now apply.

But there is great need for such stories, spreading over a wide regional area the complexities of faith through local contact.

I worked for six years in Liverpool, a redeemed cauldron of sectarian bitterness. There is a parish priest there, working among the tower block flats on the traditional border between Roman Catholic and Protestant Orange Lodge die-hards. He is also a member of the international

Anglican-Roman Catholic Commission; a group of theologians exploring in meetings around the world how to defuse the explosive theological issues which most divide the two world communities. His story is a classic example of how a complex theological issue can be explained in human terms.

A short distance away was a charismatic church I wrote about, where Roman Catholics and members of the Orange Lodge praised God together during exuberant three hour services. There were drama and personalities enough to fuel any newspaper feature; although there would be few editors willing to accept what the article was technically about, the theology of reconciliation. On the same theme, I met a young Roman Catholic at the ecumenical *Corrymeela* Community in Northern Ireland who grew up in the Catholic heartland of Belfast. He did not speak to a Protestant until he was eighteen. When he first went to *Corrymeela* he sat in a corner for a weekend and scowled. When he went home he made a vow: never to have dealings with such a place again. When I spoke with him he was a resident community member. Such people are the living theology any newspaper reader will relish.

There remain two mountain ranges after the plains of local journalism and the foothills of the provincial Press. One is the panorama of Fleet Street newspapers; the other the definition of the Church.

Increasingly Fleet Street is taking an interest in church affairs. Pope John Paul II dominated the front pages during his visit to Britain. There were more than sixty journalists and six camera crews in the Press gallery at Church House, Westminster, for the Church of England debate on the report *The Church and the Bomb*. There will always be interest in the exclusive telephoned tip as much for the church as for any other exclusive story. The novel, the intriguing, the thought-provoking and the controversial will always gain an audience. For all the organisation the churches can muster there will always be the good stories that slip through the net and a telephone call to see if they are known about is often the first step to their revelation.

The major church conferences, the special services and the large campaigns will always have advance publicity, but the intriguing detail—the divisions and controversies which the Press have as much right to expose as the triumphs—can remain hidden unless an amateur contact picks up a telephone. The national Press does also have some limited opportunities for guest writers, for the inclusion of controversial material in gossip and diary columns and for explanatory features. Such possibilities are best explored with individual newspapers. It is always best for amateur representatives of the churches to concentrate on papers with which they are familiar through their own affinities.

Meanwhile, even while we plan, the ground is moving beneath our feet. The ecumenical and charismatic movements are at work on the traditional foundations. The myths are collapsing; the caricatures erased or at least re-drawn. Traditional church worries about roofs and clergy deployment are not issues in the house churches with lay pastors. Church unity talks are by-passed where Catholic and Protestant differences are exhumed, if only locally, in the fire of the Holy Spirit. The wearing graph of decline is turning upwards; but in the least publicised aspects of the churches, the black congregations and the renewal movement often meet outside denominational divides.

There is a paradox in much present church reporting, looking, as it does, through still stained glass windows on historical practices without a guaranteed future. As links between the Church and the Press are strengthened this paradox will be brought more firmly into the public spotlight. And one of the conventions of current journalism, the reinforcement of an accepted image, will then itself come under strain.

Chapter Eight

GHOST—WRITING

By

Jane Collins

'Writing this book was a tremendously rewarding experience.'

Jane Collins is an ex-publisher trying to get her own back! After translating and tidying up other people's works, she has graduated from a grateful mention in the occasional foreword to the title page of *His God, My God,* the ghosted autobiography of Caroline Urquhart. Jane's two toddler daughters are trying to ensure this doesn't get out of hand, but she has a strong ally in her husband Tony, himself an author and publisher.

When I started to write, I was given just one piece of serious advice from an experienced author and publisher.

'Get the story down, all of it, quickly, so you know where you are going. You can always tidy it up afterwards.'

This seemed a good idea, but in practice I did nothing of the sort. As various problems came up, I began to have plans of my own as to how to tackle them: most systems were doomed to be no more than failed resolutions. So, as a self-confessed beginner, let me share those difficult areas and some of the great ideas I had, then explain why I didn't follow them.

'Ghosting' sounds to the uninitiated as though someone were dead. There may be moments in the writing of someone else's autobiography when, if you don't actually wish your co-author dead, at least you wish you'd had the sense to choose as your subject someone who was dead when you started. How much easier to cope with a passive pile of letters or diaries written in the last century than all those red scribbles over your precious latest chapter, or an apologetic 'phone call:

'I'm afraid it's all come out wrong somehow. I think we'll have to meet again.'

Yet the joy of working with someone else far outweighs these moments. The loneliness of communing with a silent typewriter for hours on end, the difficulty of finding sympathetic but incisive criticism, the continual struggle to motivate yourself without encouragement—all these problems are mitigated, if not overcome, by an understanding partner. Ghosting also gives you the opportunity to get to know in depth somebody who, presumably, has an interesting past, a life-transforming experience of God and an enthusiasm to share this with others. If you're not excited by the story when you begin, then why start? Furthermore, the plot is, in theory, written. All you have to do is pick out the bits you want.

So, buoyed up with a great optimism, you plan your first meeting with your partner. If you feel as hopelessly inadequate as I did when I started, I suggest as your agenda that you discuss, and finally agree on answers to, the following questions.

1. *What are your hopes and ambitions for the book under God?*
2. *Who is going to read it?*
3. *What do you want to tell them?*
4. *Are there any other books saying the same thing?*
5. *Is there room for yours in this competitive market?*

This may sound mercenary to the idealist, but any publisher will base a decision on your answer. To crystallise your thoughts, either map out a one sentence summary of the book, or write a blurb for the back jacket which will make the browsing purchaser put his hand in his pocket. You could do this separately as preparation for the first session together. Making a list of suggested titles each will probably cause a few laughs to break the ice, and give you something to think about while you wait for a bus. Discover what books your partner has read and enjoyed, or books similar to the one you are planning which have bored or disappointed him, and find out why. All this builds up a picture in your mind, and focuses your vision.

As I supped my coffee with Caroline and Colin Urquhart in the gracious peace of his study at The Hyde, I felt right out of my depth. The bestselling author of *When the Spirit Comes*, *Anything you Ask*, and *In Christ Jesus*, Colin had taken a major role in spearheading the charismatic renewal in this country, and now had a world-wide ministry. Surely such a spiritual giant would be testing me for unworthy motives, and finding them; sounding my spiritual depths, and not finding them. I knew Caroline had taken some time to decide she would put her story on paper: why on earth should she entrust her reputation to me? When Colin left us, I didn't feel so outnumbered, but Caroline and I were still weighing each other up. Who was going to do what in this formidable task?

Wanting to appear competent, I probably muscled in too fast and tried to take over the whole show. I dictated the method, the schedule, the structure and the tone of the book, and was generally bursting with bright ideas. It was some while before Caroline felt it was anything to do with her, I think. Then, as she gained confidence, we went painstakingly back over 'my' chapters and made them 'ours'. That first meeting, in retrospect, didn't lay the best foundations for the lovely friendship it eventually became. With each new partnership a sensitive balance of input will need to be worked out. Next time, I would still have the ideas up my sleeve, but listen hard and be much more sensitive about pulling them all out on to the table immediately.

We now return to that enticing half truth that the plot is already written. Where are you going to start, and usually more difficult, where is the end? Some stories have a natural end, but many people are so involved with the present they feel that something which happened last week must be included. It isn't necessary to finish with something too dramatic, but you need more than a whimper.

One line of thought which may help here, and at other points, is that you probably have some theme or message supporting the purely chronological story. The two should interweave and inter-act, the theme dictating to a certain extent which of the historical incidents are included. This may be obvious, but it can be helpful to ask yourself questions such as 'How does what I am saying relate to the total theme of the book? What incident illustrates this point which I feel necessary to the message?' In the matter of choosing the end, the question should be, 'Is there anything, however small in apparent significance, which rounds off or sums up the theme?'

This inter-action of story and message can also help you to structure the chapters. Life doesn't fall into neat categories, but a list of the areas you have something to say about might provide the pegs on which to hang the story, and also more obvious divisions of the material. These don't have to be explicit in the book, in fact, far better not, but your points will be clearer if you put them across one at a time, and not all jumbled together.

You also need to consider the balance of these two elements. Most Christian writing (other than the purely academic) has both story and message in various proportions. Even sermons without anecdotes or illustrations are tough going, and with a book, your audience isn't wedged into a pew with nothing better to do. Decide whether the doctrine or the experience should have the upper hand in dictating the structure, or you will get lost. Ideally they should be well mixed throughout. In autobiography, the story must hold sway, and even where there is doctrine, you need to be subtle. You don't want to make it sound as though the character is rising out of the book to harangue his readers. If anything, I tend to be too subtle.

Now, are you going to begin at the beginning? Flashbacks present a particular problem. It is a good idea to start the opening chapter with something exciting, but you need to get some background information in quickly. If this is badly handled, I find it groanworthy, and often close the book. I'm sure you know the sort of story with a powie zap first scene which really grips you for two pages. Then you read, 'As the bullets whistled over my head, I fell to thinking about the farmhouse in which I was born in 1935, the second son of Mary and Tom, the village fish-merchant.'

Somehow, action and information must be bound toge-ther in a palatable way. Each book finds its own solution, but avoid a short introduction followed by a long flashback if you want me to read on.

If you have fought through as far as this you have a start, a finish and a structure. It is a short step from there to put your synopsis down on paper. This, and a first chapter, make up the minimum package for the publisher to assess. It can be quite difficult at this point to remember that this should not be a secular process baptised, as it were, by a prayer as you post it off. The whole project needs to be steeped in prayer and accompanied by a constant examina-tion of your motives. Yet guidance often comes in the form of the publisher's decision, so how can you give yourself a good chance?

As you worked through the material, were you 110% convinced that you are telling a story which will move and teach people who know nothing about the situation? Publishers, even Christian ones, are paid to be sceptical. Although light Christian biography has a shortish life-span, there may have been a recent book covering the same area which would queer your pitch. Some stories, like a miracle healing, would make an excellent magazine article, but often don't have the weight from which to draw out a whole book. Other subjects may be too negative to sell: even if you feel that the story of your friend's faith on not being healed is a necessary counterbalance to the triumphalist brigade, the publisher may know it to be a non-starter. Unfortunately, the dice are loaded against you, especially if you and the story are unknown. If someone with a public ministry was involved at any stage, perhaps they would agree to write a foreword. Without something to make the publisher look twice, your presentation needs to be impeccable and your style riveting if you are to avoid the gaping jaws of the out-tray.

The other great function of a synopsis is to make you feel that you have things under control. When you've written one chapter you know you've done perhaps one twelfth of the book, and the way is paved for you to carry on more smoothly. Without it, there will be times when the task seems interminable and impossible.

Having said that, I see before me the first synopsis of *His God, My God*. Chapter 1 is summarised down to half a side: Chapter 10 consists of two words. Chapters 3 and 4 were completely re-jigged, the flashback reduced to half its former self and shunted along twenty pages, and two years of story and two further chapters were added to what I had originally planned. This by itself hardly accounts for the extra year it took to write: that was something to do with having another baby and taking on a full-time college course. But at least I *felt* as though I had it worked out.

Once you have a mould, you can start collecting the cement to put in it: the real stuff of life. What people did before tape recorders, I don't know. Nothing stultifies the memory and train of thought like having to repeat bits or wait until it's written down. Facts can be written out or researched beforehand, but to project what it felt like to be there, you need to have been carried there yourself by your partner's description. Mind you, I remember having to hide the recorder for a couple of sessions until a timid and self-conscious Caroline could bear to see me switch the thing on and off.

Even with a recorder, hang on to your pencil and paper. Zero the counter when you start, and write down the first question you are going to ask. Each time the subject changes, note the number of the dial and what that section is about. This allows you both to range freely wherever the impulse takes you without involving you in several hours' work tracking it down later. Having a pen in your hand also means that if a question occurs to you at a point where you don't want to disturb the flow, you can scribble it down for later.

Your own experience may or may not be much help in making the past live. On occasions Caroline was surprised to find I had captured a mood which she hadn't actually been able to pin down herself: on others I had got it woefully wrong. Sometimes this was because I was barging ahead on inadequate information, relying too much on our common experience as wives and mothers.

If your subject is a very different person from you, or one of the opposite sex, you may have a much harder job than I did. A friend of mine ghosted for a man who, when asked what someone was like, could only remember the colour of their eyes and hair, any regional accent, and very little else. This is extremely frustrating if you want to use words like self-assured, homely or diffident. Yet your job as a ghost-writer is to be the mouthpiece for someone else, so their interests are important, not just your literary ideals.

I had a really good scheme for collecting my material. I thought through the chapter in advance, worked out what questions I needed to ask, and sent them to Caroline a week before we met to allow time for thought. Factual questions like 'What could you see from your bedroom window?' could be answered in writing, the more complex or emotionally flavoured ones saved for the tape. This didn't quite work.

In practice, you can't know all you need to know to structure the chapter, without having all the material. Several times I had elaborate schemes, plausible psychological developments and conversations mapped out, only to discover that it didn't develop like that, and she never spoke to anyone about it. So, despite my neatly ordered ideal, I often found that we rambled around several angles before I could see what was needed to be included and how it could be done, and a further session was necessary to find out the details. An amazing wealth of detail is needed at some points. Where was the 'phone? Did the kids drink orange or milk? What would you be likely to talk about with this particular friend? These seem unimportant until you have based half a page on a guessed answer, and it is wrong. This may not matter to you, but does your subject feel the same way? If not, your anxiety to start writing may actually cost you time and effort in the long run.

Christians are not known for clutching their brow and moaning 'What is truth?' Yet this comes up time and again in two forms, subjective and objective.

From the subjective angle, it will already be clear that I place importance on getting back into the past, and feeling it again. Unless you can forget all the rationalisations you made about a situation afterwards, and live it again with whatever pain, confusion or rapture it first brought to you, I maintain you are distorting truth. Your readers won't recognise the kind of life they lead, will put your subject on a pedestal and despair of ever being 'spiritual' themselves. Yes, you do want to stress that God moved mightily, but were you sure of your guidance at the time?

Some people find it very difficult to take themselves back, either because they don't have that sort of introspective personality, or their memory is bad, or because the pain of living through it again is too much. Prayer together, of the relaxed, exploring kind; just thinking it through before the Lord, is a great help. I must confess to taking a few surreptitious notes in the middle of one of Caroline's long and revealing prayers! For really difficult passages, Caroline asked others to pray for protection from fear and from opening of old wounds, and experienced great freedom and security as a result. And if something you've just talked about makes you want to burst out in a song of praise, why not? You need to live the complexity and richness of the experience again unless your story is to be strait-jacketed with dogma and gasping for the breath of life. Distorting the facts to make the miracle shinier will not in the long run bring glory to God.

So much for the subjective ways in which your honesty can fail. Why would anyone want to distort objective truth in a Christian book? Well, do you feel free to invent a person who never existed just so that a train of thought can be conveyed in conversational form? You may need to do this if the person with whom such a conversation could have taken place was thoroughly objectionable: you can't say that in case they read it. Or you may wish to check it with them first, and have no idea how to get hold of them. Changing a name to preserve anonymity is accepted, but can you roll two people together, or have a compendium figure to represent a whole prayer group? I contend you can, but others would say you are then moving into the realms of spiritual fiction, or less politely, lying. On balance, I would rather have a book which 'feels' true to life and so moves, challenges and convicts the reader, than one which is historically accurate but leaves him cold.

This relates to a problem for which I have no adequate answer. Where you are describing, for example, a tension in a relationship between your subject and someone else, how do you apportion blame for it? You can't be too rude about the other person, and yet you don't want to present a distorted picture of your subject as immature, petty, short-tempered or intolerant! I was always trying to portray little tensions and foist at least some of the blame on to Colin, but Caroline was having none of it. In the end, I accepted her assertion that his new spirituality didn't come across as smug complacency, and if she were ever irritated by it, she knew it was because of lack of understanding in herself. We adopted the 'ostrich' technique: if this chapter is about what it felt like to be Caroline Urquhart that autumn, then anything we describe is purely feeling with no claim to being an objective judgement on what was happening. Caroline is very humble: with a more self-assertive person, just try to avoid the more flagrant forms of libel!

At all times the story must live. Conversations, cups of coffee, tripping over the cat—anything to paint a picture the reader can walk into. I allow myself half a page of abstractions as a maximum before some direct speech, humour, description or event. This puts a heavy burden on conversations as a medium for your message. But there again anyone can write ten pages of contentless conversation: the trick is to make them count, but keep them natural. And when you've written a few chapters, check through your 'concrete padding'.

'Do you know I drink seventeen cups of coffee in the first four chapters?' said Caroline aghast, or perhaps I should say, awash. Note the self-conscious direct speech and humour. Train yourself to read other people's narrative critically, and find out what works. Assess why something jars on you, or bores you. If it's so good you can't bear to stop and think about it, read to the end and then go back and have another inspection: this is the model you need to copy, and you can learn a lot from it.

For a start, look at the length of the sentences. This needs to vary from the five-liner for a long explanation where all the clauses are interrelated, to the snappy five-word paragraph which punches the meaning across. A long ramble of six phrases beginning with 'and' needs chopping up.

Avoid the obvious and mundane, like the verbs 'to go' and 'to be'. Consecutive sentences beginning with the same word are acceptable occasionally, for special effect, but any repetition of words should be a conscious decision. With the wealth of the English language to choose from, you have no excuses for not using synonyms. Look especially for a word used at the bottom of a page and again at the top of the next: the proofs almost certainly won't be so kind.

Even if you don't want long descriptive passages, throw in a striking adjective from time to time. What about smells, temperature, touch? The right detail every half page can transform a bald and unconvincing narrative.

Cut out the waffle. You would be surprised how much you can take out of a page without distorting the meaning, and how great the benefit of this tightening up can be. Avoid spiritual jargon, or at least explain it. 'We just really had to be broken and take our fellowship to the foot of the cross': I pity the poor non-Christian trying to make sense of that.

This rigorous examination of your prose is very time-consuming at first, but as you proceed some of it becomes automatic, and if you don't enjoy playing with words your writing will always be mediocre. The giants in the field of ghosted autobiography, John and Elizabeth Sherrill, always repay study along these lines. If you don't know the names, look at the covers of *The Cross and the Switchblade*, *The Hiding Place* and *God's Smuggler*—and learn, too, that the ghost-writer usually goes unnoticed.

One of the greatest barriers I had to overcome all the way through was my pernicious lack of discipline. My quiet time took a much higher priority for a change, because I would rather do anything than look at a blank sheet of paper. For weeks on end I would do nothing, then suddenly I once wrote four chapters in five days. You can't force creativity, but neither should you hide behind the dictum for too long at a stretch. Another hazard, I eat constantly as I write. One book and a college course put about twenty pounds on me!

Yet the love and friendship I found with so many people, especially Caroline, made writing the book a tremendously rewarding experience. The exhilaration of finally getting it right, even crying at the pain you portrayed as you read it through again, and believing that thousands will benefit from sharing vicariously in what God did in one ordinary person—this is a heady joy.

Chapter Nine

WRITING FOR A BOOK PUBLISHER

By

Robert Warner

'Christian books change lives.'

Rober Warner is a graduate of York University and while there attended St. Michael-le-Belfrey. In 1979 he became an editor at Hodder and Stoughton and from 1981 was the Religious Books Editor. In Autumn 1983 he left publishing to study theology at Oxford in preparation for the ministry. He is an editorial consultant to *Renewal*.

Setting the scene

Publishers need new authors. Their established authors are invaluable. Their backlist of steady sellers provides strength in depth. But their future success must be built on today's discoveries. And you may be one of those discoveries.

Unfortunately there are no golden rules to guarantee your discovery. If I had found them, I might have copyrighted them, and sent you a copy for an enormous fee! What I can do is set the scene, and explain the things you should consider and shouldn't do.

Christian books change lives. Their influence for good is enormous. Many more people will be reached, at depth, by a bestselling book than could ever be spoken to face to face. All of us need a regular diet of new words to build faith, bear witness and help us think more clearly. This means all of us need new authors.

But writing takes time. An enormous amount of time. To write a book will take practice, care and several drafts: the best books don't just happen in a flurry of writing paper! So if you want to write a book, you must be prepared to work at your writing. What is more, you will need to make time to read.

Learn from others. Read the best Christian books. Read the best non-Christian books too. One of Hodders' best authors spent her teenage years reading Dickens. I can never understand someone who tells me he wants to be a writer, and then adds, 'But I don't read anything, you understand. Christian books today are so dreadful!'

At Hodders, scores of unsolicited manuscripts arrived each week. We reckoned to publish about two from every thousand! The trouble, for a new author, is that a publisher has several regular sources of reliable material: his own backlist, which he can re-issue in a new format or a revised edition; his established authors, with whom he likes to develop a continuing relationship; books already published abroad, which have a 'track record'; and his own new discoveries, for a publisher is always seeking new authors.

I hope this doesn't put you off. It has been said you shouldn't try to become a writer unless you have to. But if the inner compulsion is there, then *write*.

We will consider the practical things you should do in approaching a publisher. Then I will warn you what not to do. Once these hurdles are out of the way, I will take you inside a publisher's mind, and reveal the things they look for in your manuscript.

Practical matters

First, you must find a suitable publisher. Look on your bookshelves and in bookshops. Sort out which publishers produce books you enjoy reading. Try to discover the range of subjects these publishers cover. See which have interests in the area where you want to write.

You should submit to publishers one at a time. They do not have the time to become involved in lengthy correspondence only to discover someone else has settled a contract with you. This means that some of them have a policy not to consider what are called 'multiple submissions'. It is probably best not to show too many friends your work in progress. Everyone is different, and you may receive so much conflicting advice that you are left thoroughly confused.

Having found the publisher you want to approach first, remember that publishers, like most of us, are busy people. If you have not bothered to present your material professionally, that speaks volumes. If you do not believe enough in your writing to bother, why should a publisher bother to spend much time assessing it?

So take the trouble to type your material, double spaced, on standard size paper, and on one side of each sheet. Make your chapter headings and any other headings stand out. Personally, I would advise you to use clear sub-headings and short paragraphs. These help the reader, and they also help you to discipline your argument.

What should you send? First a clear, covering letter, which introduces you, giving any background relevant to your book's potential market, describing the book itself in three or four brief sentences and listing any previous published writing, whether in books or magazines.

Together with the letter you should enclose three things: a one-page summary of the book; a two or three page outline chapter by chapter; and an appropriate sample chapter. It is rarely necessary to send a complete manuscript in the first instance.

A publisher should be able to make his initial judgement on this information. If he is interested, he will be able to give you advice before you complete the 35,000 to 65,000 words he will normally require. But do remember to send a representative chapter. It does not really help if a publisher receives a sample chapter which, the covering letter explains, is nothing like the rest of the book. Finally, as a courtesy, you may also wish to enclose return postage.

What not to do

Having got over the hurdle of presentation, some alarm bells must ring. There really is no need to tell a publisher that God has told you to write your book. If God has, then he is quite capable of telling the publisher direct. Similarly, it will not help much if your letter begins, 'You don't publish books like this, but...'. Christian publishers are particularly unlikely to publish 'new revelations', spiritualists, or books that pretend to prove that Jesus was a spaceman, a totem pole, or anything else except the incarnate Son of God.

Don't use funny inks—green and purple are particularly popular for the most unlikely manuscripts. Also avoid little sketches: unless you are extremely talented, a publisher is likely to use a professional for any illustrations.

Don't pester publishers. If they have turned a manuscript down, nothing is gained by demanding a detailed explanation or resubmitting six months later. If you do receive a turn down it is best not to mention this when approaching a second publisher. Let them make their own minds up, and do not undermine their confidence by listing your rejections.

Finally, there is usually little advantage in a foreword from a local worthy. Your mayor or rural dean may be held in the highest regard, but a major publisher is looking for an international market of many thousand copies. If you have written a book restricted to local interest, find a local publisher.

Inside the publisher's mind

Now we are over the practical details, we can enter a publisher's mind. His in-tray is creaking under the weight of this morning's submissions. How can your proposal be made to stand out? What are the questions running through his mind? We will look at six.

1. *What is the potential readership?*

To be published your book must have a market. The age, theology, denomination, and academic background of your potential readership will be considered. Help the publisher and yourself by writing for your readership, rather than trying to discover a readership when the book is finished.

Don't be so broad as to be bland. But don't be so narrow

as to exclude all readers except your friends. A major publisher will be looking for books that 'travel': to a wide national readership, to a worldwide readership in English and to a readership in translation.

2. Who will respond to the book?

It is one thing to aim at a readership, another to hit the target. This question breaks down as follows:

Is the book positive? —does it encourage the reader and build faith?

Is it genuine? —does it seem honest and real or a pious fantasy?

Is it original or derivative? —following the superb bestseller *Joni*, similar stories flooded into publishers' offices. Max Sinclair's *Halfway to Heaven* is perhaps the only outstanding book which tells a related story. It is distinctive, with its own special qualities. Most of the others were second-rate, carbon copies.

Does it build a bridge? —whatever kind of book you write, you need to capture your readers. You must meet them where they are, to take them where you want to go.

3. Can the author write?

Long words, long sentences and long paragraphs are usually deadly. As a rule, so is an endless series of 'and thens'. Some writers start crisply and then slacken and grow sloppy. Worst of all is jargon and religiosity: if your non-Christian neighbour would not understand a phrase, think twice before using it.

You need to earn the right to be heard. A good book should seize you on page one and keep you reading longer than you had planned. The style should say, 'Read me.' There should be a sense of urgency. Interest must be sustained.

Most people lead busy lives. Television, magazines and newspapers all clamour for attention. A book must demand time to be read. If a publisher falls asleep over your manuscript, when it is his job to discover tomorrow's books, it will never get into the hands of readers, and make them turn its pages.

4. Does the book have structure?

A publisher's job is to help shape your manuscript. He won't be looking for the final, polished form. But he will look for a clear structure, for the way the book develops, for a clear sense of direction with signposts for the reader. He will look for a flow that carries the reader, whether a narrative's dramatic tension, or an argument's clear progression.

Don't feel you have to cram everything into one book. It's rather like a preacher who feels no sermon is complete unless it begins in Eden, ends after the Second Coming, and squeezes in everything between. You may remember Mary Poppins' amazing holdall, that contained everything she might ever need. A rag-bag of a book, all-inclusive, rambling, full of irrelevance, is much less useful. To change the metaphor, such a manuscript is quite indigestible.

One particular kind of irrelevance should be festooned with flashing warning lights. You may not like a particular person or church. But by condemning them in print in a needless aside you may prevent from reading your book the very people you wish to reach. Imagine writing a book on forgiveness in which, in passing, you condemned one particular group as unforgiving. They might never forgive you, and even feel you had never forgiven them!

5. What is the author's future?

A good publisher will advertise, send out review copies and work in every way to promote his books. He has to decide whether your manuscript will be reviewed widely, and whether a newspaper or magazine will take an extract. He also has to assess your personal 'potential': would you be suitable for interview on radio or television? Or for a related feature near publication? He will assess whether magazines might want related articles from you, whether speaking engagements or conferences might develop, and whether special events to draw in the public and the media might be arranged, near where you live and in major cities. Finally, he may consider the manuscript's suitability for commendations from well-known authors and leaders. Rare indeed is the new author who meets all these requirements, but a good publisher needs to ask all these questions. In secular publishing this would be described as deciding whether an author is 'promotable and buildable'.

6. Will it sell?

We come finally to the church. It has been said that Christians in business should serve God and the profits . . . in that order. God is not served by a publisher going bankrupt. It is unlikely to be worth publishing a book because of what it says if no one is going to read it: the hidden treasures will stay hidden, but the publisher's investment will be money wasted.

The distinction between serving God and success is often made artificially wide. Being successful is no guarantee that God is with you. But being unsuccessful doesn't prove anything either, apart from the fact that you probably will not be in business long.

A publisher may publish an occasional book regardless of sales potential, 'because it must be published'. But he cannot stay in business with these books. They have to be exceptions, only made possible by the books that do sell.

A good Christian publisher should never publish a book just because it will sell, regardless of content. Given his first duty to serve God it is then absolutely right and necessary that he asks whether a book will sell. If he decides yours will sell well, and it does, you will be able to enjoy the delight of success together.

Realism

These are the questions a publisher must ask. By asking them yourself, you will be able to assess your manuscript much more precisely. By taking account of them, you will greatly improve your potential as a writer. Having revealed these crucial questions, a little realism needs to be injected into your quest for a publisher.

a) *Who are you writing for?*
If you are writing for yourself, that is fine. It can help enormously to sort out your ideas, or to cope with a great joy or sorrow in your life. This is a perfectly legitimate reason for writing. There really is no need to feel obliged to submit everything you write to a publisher. Certainly there is no need to feel the writing has been wasted, if you have written for this reason and then it is turned down.

If you are not sure who you are writing for, submit early. It may take several years to write a book. The disappointment of so much wasted effort can be enormous. If submission confirms you are writing for yourself, that is very helpful. If it confirms you are writing for publication, and you now have a contract, you will be able to draw on a publisher's professional expertise.

b) *Poetry and special interests*
One visit to your local Christian bookshop will confirm that there is very little market for Christian verse. Nor is there great demand for '*Christian Motorcyle Maintenance*' or '*Sacred DIY*'. A little poetry is published in some Christian magazines. A tiny trickle of poetry books is published. But publishers receive a virtual deluge of this material.

It is best to be realistic. Most versifiers are more interested in writing their own words than reading others'! Similarly, if you have a special interest, be realistic about how many other Christians are likely to share it, and how many of those would prefer to rely on the books of secular specialists.

c) *Vanity publishing*

Some people choose to pay to have their book published. There are special firms which provide this service. It clearly provides satisfaction. But I would encourage you to set your sights on publication by merit, not payment.

You need to know that major publishers are not involved in what is called 'vanity publishing'. Their decision is based on what you have written and who will buy it. You will not help and may even hinder your chances of being published by offering a contribution to the publisher's production costs.

Conclusion

It may take years to write a book. It will usually take around nine months from completion to publication. The production process goes through several lengthy stages: copy-editing, type-setting, page make-up, proof reading, printing, binding and distribution to the bookshops. The cover must be designed, the print number and price determined. The book must be sold into bookshops several months before publication, and promotion plans set in action. All in all, a book must pass through many expert hands before it finally appears on display at publication.

Techniques are never enough. There is no secret method. I have revealed to you a publisher's questions, as he decides your manuscript's fate. I have warned you what not to do. You undoubtedly need to be prepared for a lot of hard work and prayer. *The Hiding Place*, one of the best loved and bestselling Christian books did not just happen. It was written by professional writers, but it took about half a dozen drafts, detailed research and persistent prayer.

With all the ability in the world, with all the dedication and determination, with all the right techniques and the right approach, even with that something special that makes your manuscript stand out, to be a good Christian writer one other thing is crucial. A calling. With a calling you will be able to persist with the writing, and you will have the persistence to find a publisher.

'Don't write unless you have to,' is good advice. If you have to write, *then enjoy it*. There is a public out there just waiting for your books. There are needs to be met and thoughts to be clarified. This may be the age of video and television. But there is still nothing quite like a good book. And nothing quite like writing one.

Chapter Ten

DO I NEED AN AGENT?

By

Edward England

'This inside, up-to-the-minute, information makes an agent invaluable to the gifted, professional writer.'

Edward England joined Hodder and Stoughton as an editor in 1966 and was the Religious Publishing Director for nine years. He resigned in 1980 to form his own literary agency, which today looks after about ninety authors.

He is the publisher of *Renewal* and recently succeeded Michael Harper as editor. The story of his publishing years is told in *An Unfading Vision*, a Hodder Christian paperback.

What is a literary agent? 'A meddlesome middleman, coming between the publisher and author,' says a London publisher who has for years been paying below the market rates. 'I had a happy relationship with an author until the agent came along.' He does not mention that the author turned to the agent in desperation after discovering he was earning little more than half of what he should have been paid. 'That publisher,' the author says, 'was such a delightful person that I felt it wrong to mention money to him.'

Early this century a London publisher, J. M. Dent, is reported to have wept when he found that an author had sought the assistance of a literary agent on completing a life of Christ. 'And to think, Mr. Gardiner,' said Mr. Dent, hardly able to believe the news, 'that with the life of our Saviour you saw fit to employ an agent! It is more than I can bear.'

'My agent is my bread and butter,' says a professional writer struggling to bring up two small children on the income from his books. 'My publisher is concerned that I keep writing, my agent that I keep eating. I need them both.'

'We look to literary agents for a big percentage of our major books,' says a famous London publisher. 'Sometimes we think publishing would be easy if we didn't have to discuss terms with agents, but then sometimes we think publishing would be easy if we didn't have authors.'

'A literary agent is an author's business representative,' says the *Society of Authors' Representatives* in New York. 'As such, his main objectives are commercial, and it is his responsibility to protect his client's best interests.' The Society adds that while it is not his main function, the agent may act as an editorial adviser, giving the author literary criticism.

The Society lists eight main services the agent can offer his client.

1. Negotiate sale of lease of certain rights in his work.
2. Reserve rights not essential to the negotiation in hand for later disposition in other markets.
3. Examine contracts and negotiate modifications.
4. Recommend contracts for approval or rejection, stating reason.
5. Collect monies due.
6. Examine royalty statements.
7. Check on publisher's handling of a book.
8. Check on copyright.

The current *Directory of Publishing* lists sixty-four authors' agencies in Britain: there are many more. Some agencies have two or three hundred authors each linked to a director or partner of the company who may specialise in fiction, or radio and television scripts, serial sales, or foreign rights. A few agencies, including one of the most prosperous, limit themselves to a dozen or so authors. An agency cannot be judged by its size but by the flair, industry and negotiating ability of its senior staff and the quality of its authors. Many successful agents have worked in executive positions in book publishing, as magazine editors, or in television or films. They are often negotiating with former associates whose likes and dislikes they have absorbed.

Few agents deal with poetry, or plays; some do not handle anything shorter than a book-length manuscript; most are abysmally ignorant about religious writing. The dream of launching a successor to C. S. Lewis may have tempted them once to handle a bishop's Lent book but they soon discover a novelist or cookery writer has better commercial potential. My own entry into this specialist field of agency work has alerted two large agencies in London to the realisation that they may nevertheless be missing out. They are. For although religious books command small advances, and don't make the national bestseller lists, the best do go on selling and reprinting for years.

In an ideal world there would be no need for agents. A publisher would employ editors who would care for the writer's welfare as consistently as for his employer's. The editor would provide the impartial advice and the individual support which every writer needs. A few do. Indeed I have found them all more amenable than did George Bernard Shaw, who, at the annual dinner of the Society of Authors in 1906, spoke of the publisher's sweatshop: 'Those of you who, like myself, have studied "sweating" as an industrial phenomenon are aware that it occurs at its very worst in those trades where the employer, instead of having work done in his own factory, gives it out to workers who do it in their own homes.'

Seventy-five years later David Caute, recalling this speech in *The Times* wrote that publishers are still 'offering terms which are anarchically divergent and often cruelly exploitive; the current publishing crisis naturally provides an ideal alibi for turning the screw even tighter.'

At the Booker Prize award ceremony in 1983, novelist Fay Weldon attacked British publishers for their outmoded attitudes. 'Writers know well enough that they are like Atlas, bearing on their shoulders all those who depend upon them for their income, the exercise of their own skills, their status and their very jobs. Publishers, booksellers, editors, librarians, journalists, academics, festival organisers, arts councils, would be nothing without writers.

'So, to the publishers I would say this. We are the raw material of your trade. You do tend to forget it, you know. You use us, the living us, and quite frankly, you don't look after your raw material very well. And as you turn into an industry, so we must turn into workers and organise. I think you'd do without us altogether if you could, if there was a way of producing a book without writers—people who can never be trusted to produce a product of consistent quality.....I will ask you if in your dealing with authors you really are being fair, honourable, and right, or merely getting away with what you can?'

Philip Attenborough, President of the Publishers Association, rejected some of Fay Weldon's criticisms 'so liberally thrown at publishers' staffs' and with justification. But was there *any* basis for her attack?

The best Christian publishers are men and women of integrity, with commitment and vision, who see themselves as partners with writers and booksellers in proclaiming the faith. They love books, are often well-read outside their speciality, and not infrequently are engaged in ministry in their local church. They can show unbelievable patience with erring authors. Yet they can also be neglectful of a writer's financial well-being, having never been schooled to think of this as their responsibility. Their concern is for those on the payroll: office staff, warehousemen, sales representatives. The author, the life-blood of publishing, lives far away and is forgotten for months at a time. Few writers are paid as highly as packers and computer operators.

If publishers can be neglectful and authors unreliable what about agents? A famous publisher, the late Sir Stanley Unwin, of George Allen and Unwin, would thunder they too had faults. 'I have always maintained,' he wrote, 'that they should be as open to criticism as publishers are, and have pointed out that just as there are good and bad publishers, there are good and bad agents.' In his view a bad agent had special friends among publishers, 'whom they tend, probably unconsciously, to think of first, whether or not they are necessarily the best suited for the particular book being offered. Moreover, some agents have no dealings at all with some publishers of repute and vice versa.'

Do you need an agent? Probably not. Certainly not if you only write poetry or articles for church magazines, or are a beginner or a casual writer with no literary ambition. No writer needs an agent if he is satisfied with both his publisher and his earnings. Couples with perfect marriages do not need marriage guidance counsellors.

An agent is unlikely to find you a publisher for a manuscript which has already been turned down by everyone you can think of; he is unlikely to try. An agency is no refuge for beginners. It is often the author who has had one book published, or one television play transmitted, who needs an agent more than the writer struggling to get a first step on the ladder.

Agents deal with writers who are making it and have potential for more ambitious projects; whose books deserve to be published in America as well as Britain, and should be translated into other languages. Agents are at home with those publishers whose books are well represented in public libraries and in the High Street bookshops. Agents encourage creative talent, growing literary output, and occasionally make it possible for writers to earn a living with their pen. A high percentage of authors published by major secular publishers work through an agency. If your writing is exclusively for a small denominational press, or a missionary society, it is unlikely that you need an agent.

Who needs an agent? Regularly published authors who are mystified by small print clauses in publishers' contracts. Authors who cannot bear to question the terms which a publisher offers at the end of a pleasant lunch. Normally the writer of a first book whose work is of international significance or is likely to attract media attention.

I rarely see a contract from a publisher with standard terms which I could recommend an author to sign. Contracts are weighted in a publisher's favour; after all he prepared them. It may simply be a question of deleting a few clauses, or of adjusting the royalty rate, or proposing a bigger advance. If a publisher is accepting a book with some hesitation it is not unreasonable for him to offer modest terms, and he will; but he may also offer them for the potential bestseller to compensate for the books he has published in error. Some publishers, not all, offer the minimum for a border-line book and the minimum for a major book. An agent will question this.

A responsible agent, and the rest don't survive, does not seek to negotiate contracts which are unjustly tipped in the author's favour. He attempts, from a middle position, to establish a fair balance between the two partners, to reach an amicable agreement.

The contract a publisher will propose to an agent may differ significantly from the one he offers directly to an author.

An agent does not demand outrageous advances or royalty rates. Publishers must survive and make profits to finance next year's books. He is accustomed to publishers who offer too little (most do), but he has also met writers who expect too much.

Gary Provost, an author of five books and over a thousand stories and articles in more than fifty magazines and newspapers, warns authors not to expect their agent to market every manuscript they submit. 'One of the most valuable services an agent can provide is to tell you your book stinks.' He points out that if an agent sent out every manuscript he received he would be worthless to his clients. 'The whole value of agents, from an editor's point of view, is that agents are sending only material which they rate highly and which they believe will interest that particular editor. In other words, the manuscript has been screened by a pro.'

Most established agencies discourage unsolicited manuscripts except from published authors, although they will respond to brief outlines. Others, particularly in America, will read a manuscript for a fee which is refunded if the manuscript is placed. Agents recruit new talent by recommendations, referrals from editors, or direct solicitation.

Some agents will not take on a writer until his annual

writing income is more than £2,000 or even £5,000, which is why few agents have an interest in religious titles where earnings are traditionally low and lower than they should be.

Here are some extracts from agents' handouts. 'Potential clients must be highly recommended by someone we know. We read unsolicited queries from established writers'; 'Must be professional'; 'Must be of proven competence as a writer'; 'Prefer that new authors send a comprehensive chapter outline, background data on himself, and the first four chapters of his manuscript'. If this seems to add up to an agency offering help to those who don't need it one American agency does advertise bravely, 'Prefers to work with talented newcomers.' Even this agency however expects *all* manuscripts to arrive with the return postage. If only they did!

If you have high aspirations to develop your writing skills, then demonstrate your motivation by getting an article or two published in national magazines or newspapers or prepare a detailed synopsis of your proposed book with specimen chapters.

What does an agency charge for its services? Normally, a commission of 10% on British sales, 15% on USA sales and 20% on translations. (Note: if there is no agent and the publisher handles the sale of American and translation rights he may keep anything from 19% to 50%). Some agencies have slightly higher rates which can be justified where there is considerable work for modest returns. If an author's income is in hundreds rather than thousands the agent is unlikely to cover his overheads, e.g. office expenses, postage, travel, entertaining.

What does an agent look for when selecting a publisher? He is concerned with far more than the advance payment and the royalty rate. A high royalty is of little use if the publisher does not sell any books. There are publishers who love their books so greatly that they are happy to let them rest permanently in their warehouses. If someone sends an order they service it but they do little marketing or promotion. It is not sufficient to have a book published. It has to be produced attractively, at a competitive price, launched with publicity, and be available in the bookshops on publication day. The agent knows that an identical book can sell 5,000 copies with publisher A and 15,000 with publisher B.

The agent is attracted to publishers who make an editorial input. This may consist of gentle direction as a book is being written or a constructive readers' report when it is finished. He will be wary of publishers who are not satisfied with any manuscript until their editor has reconstructed it. There are publishers, especially in America, like that.

There are publishers who accept manuscripts and then fail to publish for two or three years. A book should normally be in the bookshops within nine to twelve months of the manuscript being finalised. Under-capitalised publishers with cash-flow problems cause heart-ache here: they simply run out of money. While the manuscript gathers dust in the office it loses its topicality or is overtaken by a book from another publisher. An agent will ask for a publication date when clinching a deal.

An author may be content to have his manuscript accepted; an agent will ask the size of the first printing. This will vary from publisher to publisher. The publisher may explain to the uninitiated that the print number is unimportant—he can reprint quickly—but if the retail price, as is customary, is based on the costing of the initial print, it may be so high that the book will be doomed. A lower retail price would have given it a chance.

What can an agent offer (if he makes an offer at all)? Inside knowledge. He will be acquainted with what other authors are being paid. He will not be at liberty to share this but it will determine his expectations. He will be able to compare a contract you are offered with hundreds of others he has negotiated. He will have authors of colour illustrated books who may get as little as 5% or 6½% of the retail price, and others who receive 15% for a hard cover book. He will know that with some publishers the advance is more important than the royalty rate and that with others the advance is secondary.

His inside knowledge will extend from individual con-tracts to the fortunes of publishing houses. Even Christian publishers go into liquidation, making heavy losses for authors as well as printers. He will be aware of which publishers delay cheques, and which pay promptly. There are authors who have waited months and even years for monies due to them. Chasing overdue payments is the most tiresome part of his job, but he discovers which publishers to avoid.

With religious books he is sensitive to those who favour evangelical or liberal manuscripts; charismatic or reformed; theological or experience-centred, and the subtle differences between the Hodder and Stoughton religious list and that of William Collins, both general publishers.

Because he is in communication with most leading publishers he will know which have too many manuscripts and which are looking for a blockbuster for Christmas. The publisher will have signalled his needs for contributors to a series or for a ghost-writer for a personality biography. This inside, up-to-the-minute, information makes an agent invaluable to the gifted, professional writer.

A good agent will foster the relationship between an author and an editor. While he will negotiate all business matters, he believes the author and editor should regularly share in the development of a book from its conception to publication day. No editor can cope with an author who constantly calls, writes, or telephones, but an editor is part of the creative process and a good one is priceless.

If your agent strongly recommends A, do not insist he first tries every publisher from B to Z. I had that experience and finished back with A, but months were wasted and considerable postage. If the agent is going to take 10% of your income before sending your royalties on to you, let him advise and work for it. It is in his interest to obtain the best deal for you, to secure the right publisher—who may not be the biggest. If the agent fails to please you with the first book do not offer him the second. Most agents do not want you to sign a two or three book contract with them. It is a book at a time. You leave them if you are dissatisfied; they say goodbye if they find you are impossible. Partings are surprisingly rare.

There are a few authors who think of nothing but the size of their royalty cheque. They should not be writing spiritual books. There are publishers who think of little but profits. They should leave Christian titles alone. Likewise the Christian agent will be sensitive to those situations where he should not press for every advantage, benefit or return for his client knowing he must 'seek first his kingdom and his righteousness'.

The oldest literary agency founded in 1875 recently declared: 'At no time have authors needed the services of a literary agent more than today.' In recent years I have found how true that is.

Chapter Eleven

HOW A WRITER SEES

By

Jenny Cooke

'Seven-eighths of the iceberg'

Jenny Cooke is married with three children. As well as being a writer she teaches Lipreading and Creative Writing at her local Adult Education Centre. She also contributes to *Renewal* Magazine. Her first major book is *The Cross Behind Bars*, the biography of Noel Proctor, Prison Chaplain, in the Christian bestseller lists for many months. At the moment she is working on her autobiography.

'It's not how a writer writes *about the world that first counts. It's how a writer* 'sees' *the world that first counts.'* (Bill Stanton)

I have always loved words. I learned to read before I went to school and can still remember sitting bored in the Infants' classroom while everyone else chanted lists of phonic sounds chalked on the blackboard. When our family joined Batley Public Library, it was nothing to me to read three books in an evening: two 'Enid Blytons' sandwiched round a book on horses.

My parents moved to Macclesfield when I was thirteen. Soon studying for my 'O' Levels swamped everything. One day I took my text-book, *Poetry For Fifth Forms* and wandered to the canal bank in the High School grounds. The minutes seemed to flip by and there was the school bell. I frowned and looked at my watch. Over half an hour had passed and I'd been so absorbed in the poems that time was forgotten.

I became drunk with words. With the 'World charged with the grandeur of God' of Gerard Manley Hopkins; with 'that one talent which is death to hide/lodged with me useless' by John Milton; and with the sonnets of John Donne. 'Batter my heart three-personed God' spun round my mind. Safe with such poets' view of a world ruled by God, I rested easily.

Once I wrote an essay in great fervour for my English

teacher. It was about a warehouse full of materials: gold lace, silks and satins tumbled out onto the page. When she handed me back my work I was eager to see my mark. But there was no red pen at the end of the last paragraph. She asked me to wait behind at the end of the lesson. 'You see,' she said slowly, 'I couldn't mark it. I couldn't decide if it was very good...or very bad.'

'Oh I see,' I replied. But I didn't. Not at all.

One day I switched on my radio and happened to hear most of a play, about Russians whose names were mouthfulls of consonants. My head reeled for over twenty-four hours with the memory of it. I had thought only Shakespeare wrote plays! The curious, mournful atmosphere of the play and the sadness of the characters not finding what they were looking for filled me with an excitement I didn't understand. I searched through the pages of the *Radio Times* to find the title. *The Seagull* it said. By Anton Tchehov.

In my Sixth Form I had a wonderful teacher called Isabel Dent, who passed on her love of words, her supressed excitement about language, particularly about Shakespeare. Then in my final year at school I discovered the works of modern, existentialist writers like Jean-Paul Sartre and Samuel Beckett. Theirs was no rich splurge of language cascading over the page. It was sparse and devastating. As I read about Vladimir and Estragon waiting, endlessly, for Godot, I was filled with a pity and an anger. All of a sudden I dropped God from my thinking. If such writers had, then I would too. This made me no happier, but I felt considerably more grown-up.

During my Leeds University days I studied English Literature, but by the Second Year began to quail at the book list of over two hundred books to be ploughed through that year alone. Somehow we swapped second-hand copies amongst friends and read them all. Yet the weight of it made me dry up inside. I wanted to read translations of Cervantes, Rabelais, Homer, Descartes—and Womens' Magazines—all in a glorious muddle and all at once. But there was nothing like *that* on the book list. Even today I still like to read several books at once and leave them in piles round the house.

During the Second Year I began to write oodles of poetry, or really prose-poems about the beauty of Nature and my sorrow that life seemed meaningless. Then there was the beginning of a novel which was kept in an otherwise empty drawer in my room. Once I knew my friends were out of the way I pulled it out and wrote and wrote. It was full of themes and symbols and young love untying knots in relationships. By the end of the fourth chapter I knew it was no good.

However one book on the book list did speak to me. We were set a ten thousand word vacation paper on Milton's epic poem, '*Paradise Lost*'. At twelve books long it was some poem to read, let alone write about. So it was packed in my suitcase and taken on the family holiday to Highcliffe-on-Sea. My father was quite amazed when he brought me a cup of tea in the mornings to find me bent over the pages before breakfast. Gradually the story of Adam and Eve gripped me. What I had rejected in the Bible as being ridiculous, came across with force from Milton's pen. It didn't make me believe in God again. But reluctantly my mind acknowledged the existence of this Christian world-view and I found I respected it.

By now my inspiration as a writer was drying up and I knew it. So I packed away my poems in a brown paper envelope and pushed in the novel as well. Then the whole lot went to the back of a drawer and was forgotten.

The Third Year at University was weighed down by exams. I found little pleasure in books anymore, but struggled with the learning of Anglo-Saxon, the understanding of Literary Criticism and the unravelling of Henry James. I made a new friend called Sue Harris in the English Department and we had friendly discussions about politics over dinner. Later I found out that she was a Christian and that surprised me.

Then there were the times and times I walked the evening streets of Leeds, or tramped round the City Art Gallery, questioning and questing in my mind. Was there a God? Was there? I didn't particularly want to ask that question but it beat in my brain and popped up when I least expected. And no one apparently knew the answer. Or cared.

Finally, out of desperation, I accepted Sue's invitation to come to a Bible Study meeting in our Hall of Residence. I went reluctantly—but came out deciding to at least try the Christian Way once more.

Over the weeks something drew me on. I went to more groups. To church services. I started to pray. Then one day I opened a drawer and found the brown paper envelope full of poems and the forgotten novel. I stared at them and then flicked through them. I wished I could start to write again, but knew I'd nothing to say, nothing to compel me to get out the paper and pencil. As my fingers played over the pages, I caught a hint of a voice in my mind's ear. 'Don't write now,' it seemed to say. 'Let go of it for me.' I sighed and the papers flipped back into the drawer. It would be no great sacrifice after all. I knew I had nothing left to say. As I was closing the drawer there was that faint whisper of a voice again: 'One day, many years from now, you will write...'

'Pardon?'

It came again, slightly louder, 'One day, many years from now, you *will* write..'

I stood still for a long time pondering. Had God called me? There was no doubt he could have done. Only I wasn't sure I'd heard him correctly. And as the days went by, that almost imperceptible voice slipped to the back of my mind.

So I grew up and left the University. I went to teach in a school for the deaf. I married a wonderful man. And I forgot the world of books. So crushing was the weight of that final University year, with its endless books and poems to force down that my love of reading died. For seven years afterwards I rarely bought a book, never went to a library and never read anything from one week to the next.

For four years in the Royal Residential Schools for the Deaf at Cheadle Hulme I struggled. And struggled. The children struggled and strove as well. I was enmeshed in the work, in trying to teach them to speak, to give them an approximation of language.

It's only on looking back I realise I was learning other things as well, quite unconsciously. I was learning about the roots of communication, about the importance of words. I had to strip my mind of years of intellectualism, of words like 'epitome', 'metaphysical', 'world view', 'concept' and 'simplistic'. I had to rid myself of using Christian words like 'redemption', 'salvation' and 'atonement'. They were all useless for these children. Anything woolly or vague had to go. Only the most concrete of concrete words were any good.

I had to relearn my use of language. This was hard. Once I decided to teach my second year Infants class about colour and planned to limit myself to the three primary colours. All the other colours, their subtle nuances of shade and tone would be too complex. So I got three plastic hoops, one red, one yellow and one blue and put them on the classroom floor. Then I asked the children to find the right coloured objects and put them in the correct hoop. After they had done that I was going to teach them the written words: *red, blue, yellow.*

Not one child moved. They stared back at me, their sun-burned faces puzzled, their eyes anxious and a little fearful. I explained again. One or two blonde heads turned. Someone giggled.

Then the penny dropped. I'd made it too hard. Sighing inwardly, I swept away the blue and the yellow hoops. 'We'll do "red"' I said. 'We'll find everthing that's red in the classroom.' There was a pause. 'Everything else is, er "not-red".' It worked. They understood. Three weeks later they'd finally grasped the three primary colours.

That same year the headmaster brought a new girl called

Claire down to my classroom. 'Do your best with her will you?' he said, and turned to go, casually calling back over his shoulder, 'By the way, she's got no language at all. No words. Can't even make a noise.' Long after his footsteps died away down the corridor, Claire and I looked at each other. I took her hand and she stood stiffly beside me.

For nine months I tried to teach her to speak, to laugh, to make a noise. She was obedient and opened and closed her mouth in copy of mine. But it was all meaningless to her. She'd no concept of a word; no way of understanding that a movement of my mouth referred to an object in the room. Day in and day out I tried. But her brain just didn't 'get' it.

Then one morning her mother sent a parcel. As we started to open it I suddenly heard a voice I'd never heard before in that classroom. 'Home! Home!' called the voice. I glanced at all the children. Who on earth was talking? Then I saw Claire. She was standing up and trembling with eagerness. She looked as if someone had switched on a light inside her head. 'Home!' she called and ran to her parcel. It had happened at last. She'd 'learned' her first word. In the next six weeks she learned to speak fifty-three new words with understanding. And without my knowing it, I was building up my own 'word-hoard'.

In those years I learned to use the question: the How? Where? What? When? and Who? Without my knowing it the seeds of being able to interview people were being planted in me. I was learning to listen to the cadences of ordinary speech and this helped later when I came to write dialogue. I was discovering how to break down language to its very bones: to disorganised sounds and involuntary tongue movements. And then build it up again, slowly, so slowly. I discovered language was so much more than its component parts: its syllables and consonants and vowels. These were its raw materials. But language was meaning and life, even as a melody was more than notes and a picture more than colours.

I read a book called *English for the Rejected* by David

Holbrook. I didn't take it in as I should have done but the title was eloquent and stayed with me. Those multiple handicapped and deaf children in my class needed any English I could give them. It was the concrete nouns like *cow, pig* and *sheep* or verbs like *run, walk* and *jump* that made sense to them.

It came to me that I had once read that *cow, pig* and *sheep* were Anglo-Saxon words. When the Normans invaded England in 1066 A.D. they brought French and its Latin roots into our native Anglo-Saxon tongue. When *cow, pig* and *sheep* were served at Norman feasting tables by Saxon serfs, the meats were called *beef* (boeuf), *mutton* (mouton), and *pork* (porc). French was the posh language used by the nobility, Anglo-Saxon the language of the under-dog. So began the double strain in our English language, of Anglo-Saxon on the one hand and Latin on the other. It's given us a rich language. But old customs die hard. Intellectuals still like to use long, Latinate words. And slang and dialect are often short, strong words, rooted in Anglo-Saxon and Norse. I, in my 'English Lit.' tradition had 'majored' on the Latinate. My little deaf children began, unconsciously, to make me reach back to the older language.

Once as University students, we all went into the lecture hall and the lecturer opened a book and began reading in a foreign language. I listened, puzzled, but then excited. I felt I knew it. I'd heard it before somewhere. As if in a dream or half memory, I couldn't quite grasp it . . . . . . if only he'd read a bit slower. Suddenly he stopped and snapped the book shut. 'That was Anglo-Saxon, that was!' he boomed and the room collapsed in giggles. But the memory stayed with me. I half guessed my roots as a language-user lay there.

Eventually I left the School for the Deaf and began to raise my own family. At a time when I should have been happy and fulfilled with my young son and baby daughter I knew myself to be deeply unhappy and frustrated. The years crawled by and still I was searching for that 'something' I hadn't yet found. Perhaps, after all, there was nothing to find. And my sadness increased.

Then one day out of the blue, Michael Harper, editor of *Renewal* Magazine, rang me up and asked me to expand a letter I'd written in to the magazine and make it into an article. I did so and it was published. I did another article. And another. By the time I'd posted the second one I'd discovered I'd been thoroughly happy while writing it. And I began to wonder: supposing writing were the 'thing' I'd been searching for?

Ideas long forgotten floated to my surface again: my love of poetry and plays; my poems and unfinished novel in the brown paper envelope; the value of reading; my parents egging me on to become a journalist like my Great-Grand-father who'd worked on the *Hull Daily Mail*; the voice half-heard in my student room, 'One day, many years from now, you will write...'

In those seven years between leaving University and beginning my first article I'd trodden, without realising it, an important path. I'd read little and written less, but I'd learned at close hand the bedrock necessity of communication, the need to have something to say, to care about words, to have layers and layers of interest in language. And I was having an emerging sense of call to the work.

Even more important I was learning to care for people, to develop relationships and build a home as a place where caring flowered. Later as a fully-fledged writer I discovered how vital it is to have compassion on my characters and to care for the people I am writing about. I may like them very much or not at all, I may approve of them or disapprove of them. I may have to be merciless in exposing some truth or evil that needs dealing with. But the true artist always cares for his people as he works. As indeed God does with us.

No experience is wasted to the writer. It all becomes the humus, the soil, the melting pot in the subconscious; the hidden depths of the personality; a hoard of words, ideas, emotions, perceptions and interests. It is the seven-eighths of the iceberg. If there were no seven-eighths below the surface, there'd be no eighth above. If there are no hidden depths to the writer, there is no writer.

'It's how a writer "*sees*" the world that first counts.'

References

Anton Tchehov, 'The Sea-Gull from *The Cherry Orchard and the other Plays* trans. by Constance Garnett (Chatto and Windus 1950).
Samuel Beckett, *Waiting for Godot* (Faber and Faber).

Chapter Twelve

HAVING SOMETHING
TO SAY

By

Jenny Cooke

'It excites me to remember that God gives us language and speaks to us in a Book and in books.' *Peggy Noll*

'It excites me to remember that God gives us language and speaks to us in a Book and in books.' (*Peggy Noll*)

'First have something to say. Then write it down as clearly as you can. That is the basis of style.' (Attributed to Matthew Arnold.) Having something to say is the single most important factor for any writer. It can be anything; a feeling, a story, a desire to catch a mood in words. It could be a grief about a sick relative, a sharing of your faith, some beauty of Nature to be shared. It can be in any form; poem, play, article, novel and so on. 'Having something to say' is a something that creeps up your back. It won't go away. It's insistent and increasingly urgent to be said.

Once I wanted to write a story. I knew a story was waiting to be told. But I had to wait five years until I knew what the story was. In the end my 'story' was written in play form about some Russian refugees sent back from England after the end of the last war.

For me serious writing began with the writing of poems. I showed my first one to my friend, Sue Talbot. She pondered the text of '*Whitbarrow Scar*' — *1975:*

> Old and other,
> You stand.
> Before I was, you were
> And will be, when I am gone.

144

Ancient, dun-gray, massive hill,
You endure;
Sphynx-like,
Shoulder hunched to the wind....

After the intensity of burning words onto the paper, it wasn't easy to bring out a piece of work into the cold light of day. It was even less easy to ask a friend for her opinion. However Sue liked it, encouraged me and gave me some advice: 'Do more,' she said, 'and learn about paring your work down. Pare it, pare it and pare it again. Make all your words count. Make them work.'

I've often thought back to this little incident. An encouraging voice from a friend can open up new avenues. But if the voice is cold, even jealous, it can take a lot to regain confidence. Not all criticism is good criticism, though some may be of a fine quality and need listening to. So I'm careful to whom I show my work. And even more considerate when people ask me for my opinion. 'Tread carefully,' goes the old saying, 'for you tread on my dreams.'

At the same time as writing poems I began to get excited by certain ideas. What was the role of women in the home? In the church? In the world of work? What about creativity? And the dark night of the soul? Was there such a thing as a 'theology of childbirth'?

Michael Harper, and later Tom Smail, as editors of *Renewal* Magazine, were encouraging and kept printing my articles. This helped to build up my feeling that perhaps, and it was only perhaps, writing was going to be a biggish part of my life.

I'd known all along that unless there was 'Something to Say' I might as well not bother. As one article was posted, I used to worry and ponder whether the springs would dry up inside and there'd be nothing left to say. But somehow there always was something and another article always on the brew. As long as I wasn't in too much of a hurry and allowed my mind time to range over ideas, then ideas came.

Being a housewife had its advantages. My mind and heart had lots of time to range, while my hands got on with cleaning and cooking. It must be difficult to allow yourself that kind of time if you are tied to a desk all day and every day. Perhaps the necessary pressures of family life were the cause of Elizabeth Gaskell's reputed reply to a young writer who asked her the secret of her success. 'Well, first you must learn to make a good casserole,' said the novelist and mother of five children.

Then there were the stories. I wanted to write down the stories of people's lives—their struggles and their faith. Not necessarily the ones that neatly fitted into theological statements, or evangelical language or charismatic moulds. But the stories of 'ordinary' folk. There was the story of my friends who adopted what the doctor called a 'deaf vegetable'. And the child grew into normality. Then the story of my husband's redundancy. There were so many. I realised in the end that everyone who's ever lived has a story to tell, if only someone will listen or write. And I wanted to tell these stories.

The best way of tackling this was to wait until I was ready and then splurge it all down in longhand. Getting ready could involve me in interviewing with a portable tape recorder; checking facts in the library; sometimes in looking up words in a Hebrew Dictionary. At different times a local historian, a university lecturer and a Consultant doctor all helped me check and double check my facts. I had to be as sure as I could be that I had the correct facts and that I understood them. In an effort to find Truth, it's so important to get at truth and truths. There's no honour to anyone if this 'getting ready' stage is rushed.

Eventually I'd be ready and know it. Then to pour it down. A piece of work would emerge in a form that appealed and seemed suitable, usually an article or story. This was the excitement. I'd type it, check it and post it. Then I'd wait for the lonely excitement, the words printed on the page, and possibly even letters to the editor about my work.

But…and this as I look back, was the great divide. I became dissatisfied. I was having 'something to say'. Writing it down as 'clearly as possible' and getting it published. But what about 'the basis of style'?

I'd joined a Poetry Workshop at the Wilmslow Guild run by the poet, Harold Massingham and submitted work for weekly discussion. This was nerve-racking but vital as local poets pored over each others' work. It was a secular atmosphere but I loved it and felt at ease there. Under Harold's sensitive leadership people talked at length about their wrestling with words. They shared their questing and questioning about life. And death. And always the discussion came back to the struggle to find the right word, the 'mot juste', the word hunt.

One evening I handed in my first poem with a 'Christian' subject:

> I thought to follow Christ would mean
> A dull routine of Sunday best,
> Unperceptive talk about the status quo,
> a loss of stature and a thrust of tracts,
> unworthy prayer, unlovely clothes:
> a safe reduction to the middle way.
>
> But found, despite these reliquaries,
> He was a self both good and terrible.
> Demanding the first place. Giving
> experience zeniths. Seeming capricious,
> Yet not so. Yearning to be found
> And reflected in his followers:
> As ancient tapestry, when worked with gold
> reflects the sunshine through the leaded lights.

My stomach became a knot at first I read it aloud and then waited in silence for the verdict. Would they think I was daft? At last Harold roused himself and opened his mouth to speak, but another man interrupted, 'Why on earth haven't you shown us this before? It's your best work!'

My knees felt strange and I knew they were being kind. But obviously they didn't think I was daft. There was a very long pause, then Harold said quietly, 'It's perfectly clear from this poem that Christ is your passion.' I waited, hardly daring to breathe.

He looked at me for some moments and then at the poem again. 'You *must* write about him. You *must*. I mean it.' I was so astonished I couldn't speak. Then I stammered out, 'But...I thought...you might think I was...preaching at you...and so I didn't...', I floundered to a stop.

'Well? Are you preaching?'

'Er, no. Not at all. The last thing on my mind.'

'That's O.K. then. Don't worry about it. It's your intention that counts.'

There was another long silence. And then Harold smiled. 'I want to see at least fourteen more poems on this, er, "Christian" subject!' he said.

I couldn't say another word for the rest of the evening, even while the others debated my poem. To have my secret longing so unusually perceived and confirmed by a writer whose volumes of poetry were on sale in good bookshops was overwhelming. I tore to the bus-stop on my way home with a song bursting out of the corner of my mouth.

But still I wasn't satisfied. One evening as I led my own students at Night School in a Creative Writing Class, it suddenly dawned on me that I needed a teacher myself. Someone to teach me the craft of writing. After all a person who wanted to be a doctor or a teacher, for example, wasn't allowed to practice until he had had years of training and passed exams. So if I wanted to be a writer, shouldn't I search for a good teacher?

The answer to my search for a good teacher came in the person of Bill Stanton, of the Writers' Consultancy Service, himself a successful writer of Radio 4 plays, and novels. I was struggling to write a *Grove Booklet* on 'Childbirth' at the time and so I began to send off monthly instalments to him and he replied on tape.

The results were quite devastating. I had, said Bill, a lot of faults; those usually shown by beginners. He detected what he called my 'English Lit.' approach. There was nothing wrong with English Literature, everything right in fact. But, he said, when the famous writers of the past wrote, they wrote freshly for their times. We had to do the same today and find a language appropriate for people brought up on the media, with its visual and aural methods.

Then there were my over-long sentences, vast paragraphs and woolly thinking, disguised with intellectual words and Latinate phrases. If you want to reach the great world outside, said Bill, who will read it? Only the 'converted' and there's plenty of books for them! You do want to reach the great world outside, don't you?

I pondered. His words hurt. But I accepted their truth. I was going to have to do a lot of thinking and a lot of rewriting of first drafts. Writing was work. Very hard work.

Bill pushed me on. Over those months I rewrote the ten thousand words of that 'Childbirth' Booklet. I changed, for example these two sentences:

> Until my first child, a son, was born I had held the rather facile assumption that as we were a Christian couple and believed that God loved us, that he would ease our path and bless me in this traditionally painful experience. Unfortunately the reality of that birth did not come up to these expectations.

I rewrote them and they became:

> Until my first child, a son, was born, I naively presumed God would make things easy for me because he loved me. But when the birth came it was so difficult that even the doctor apologised.

When the Booklet was finished I knew it wasn't perfect. But I knew I'd done my best at that particular time in my life. Bill liked part of the result. 'After all,' he said casually on the tape, 'your Christ is worth writing well for.'

His remark stayed in my mind. My Christ was worth

writing well for. So I began to work two or three hours each week day on my writing. I realised it was vital to link my call with my craft. The call and opportunities were constantly beckoning. But the craft, the craft, was a force to be reckoned with. Unless I dedicated myself to mastering the craft, my call would remain largely unpolished and fallow. Wasted and hidden.

Yet I was the mother of three children. So much of my struggle lay in the problem of finding time. But time can be found, I discovered, if one is determined. Time during the night sometimes. Or as a baby slept in the afternoons. Excuses like, 'I've got to *feel* like writing before I can start,' became meaningless. I had no such luxury. If I had a patch of time, I must use it.

I got to know Edward England and he encouraged me to write my first full-length book, the biography of the Prison Chaplain, Noel Proctor. Much as I longed to write Noel's story I nearly turned it down. 'Why?' asked my husband. 'Why, when you've waited so long to write a proper book, why are you going to turn it down?' I blew my nose. 'I really don't have the time to do a major work...' He drew himself up to his six foot height. 'Well I'm *not* going to let you turn it down. You're doing it. You don't pray about writing all these years only to turn it down in the end!' I smiled a watery smile. 'Alright then. If you say so.'

And so I began Noel's story. At times I forced my legs upstairs, tread after tread, to work on transcribing tapes. Or I forced my hands to write as the clock crept upto midnight. Often I'd sit at my typewriter in our bedroom and flex my hands. My writers' bump ached on my middle finger, but the writing flowed. Despite the weight of the work I was deeply satisfied. I bent my will to the task and discovered it was possible. Difficult but possible.

If I simply cared for my family and did my writing it was possible. There was room for no other activities during that biography. Parents and friends helped. A lovely girl called Alison Powell worked for me in the afternoons and we kept

Sundays free of work. Somehow the biography was finished. Then I gave myself and my family a quiet year to recuperate and potter in. There were no deadlines. It was even possible to begin watching television again in the evenings. I trod on my ambition to begin another book straight away and in the wake of that came a peace and quietness. A time of waiting for my next book.... I understood only too well now why Elizabeth Gaskell had told an aspiring writer to 'be able to make a good casserole'.

A helpful way of looking at my writing I found was to see it simply as work God called me to do, rather than be euphoric and talk of Great Art. It's work, much the same as a stone-mason, a cabinet maker, a painter or a weaver might do. First there's the raw material: the stone, the wood, the paints, the wools and cottons. In my case, the experience of life and its words. Then there's the idea complete in the mind's eye. The angel trapped in the stone waiting to be freed; the Persian rug design; the polished carved chair. Lastly there's the marrying of the two, the bringing together of raw material and idea. For the writer the longing to tell the story together with the craft of writing.

It's no coincidence that Jesus was a carpenter. He must have been used to taming wood into shape. I've often watched my husband wrestling with bits of wood in the garage, getting out the ruler, going to the half millimetre, learning patience and perseverance until he gets it exactly right. One of his moments of pride was when he was accepted to become a member of The Guild of Master Craftsmen.

When I was writing the Noel Proctor book I often had the mental image of myself running round a huge, twelve or thirteen foot block of stone. That was my raw material: the life, work and words of the man and his wife. I was running hither and thither sculpting it into shape, even climbing a ladder at times to reach the top better, selecting a tool here and there for the job; a paragraph of narrative, a strong verb, an extra scene. It was hard work, never perfect. Perhaps this is why some writers I've heard of, call themselves wordwrights, or wordsmiths. But one aims always for perfection, to love God with all the mind, heart, soul and strength.

Two main areas were underlined to me as I worked on this book. One was about truth, the other about the story. Evangeline Patterson, the poet, said, 'Poetry is a precision instrument for getting at the truth.' Any truth we write about can only reflect upon the man who said, 'I am the Truth.' When I wrote the 'Childbirth' Booklet my friend Peggy Noll said, 'Tell the truth about childbirth.' And I tried to, for good and for difficulty. It meant I couldn't fall into any one accepted criteria of ideas. I had to stand on my own and work out what I really thought. It means double checking all facts, all sources and all people involved. It means following one's integrity and one's intuition. If I'm not sure of something it means saying so. It takes time and trouble but it's absolutely necessary. It's what the half millimetre is to the cabinet-maker. It means being willing to admit you are wrong. It's an honourable way and perhaps the only way for the committed writer.

Then there's the story, the story and only the story. I discovered I didn't need to preach. The story could do the work for me. Let the story speak, Bill would say.

One of my first efforts was an autobiographical novel. It opened like this:

> Gemma stood in the playground uncertainly. This was the moment she hated the most. All the other children were absorbed, kicking a football, or else chanting to a skipping rope, or playing chasing and tig. They seemed so contained and assured in their groups that Gemma had not the confidence to join in, yet she was so desperate for a friend that she could not be indifferent. So timidly she hovered near a wall, trying to look as if she were engrossed in a game of solitary Jacks, so that no one would ever know or even suspect her misery.

After Bill read it he taught me about the difference between narrative and scene. The narrative *tells* the reader; but the scene *shows* him. As in a play the scene allows the reader to *see* the character being sad, happy etc. etc.. It doesn't *tell* him. An actor acts out his sadness or happiness while his dialogue may be about something quite different and will inevitably move the play forward. An actor doesn't turn round to the audience and say, 'Oh by the way, I'm sad you know!' He lets the audience *see* his sadness.

In my opening paragraph I'd worked with narrative and with the view point of an adult woman, Latinate words to match. If I were writing it now I'd try to make this paragraph into a scene, cut out as much of the 'Latin' as I could and try and enter the world of a nine-year-old child. So it might read like this:

> Gemma stood in the playground and looked about her. Everywhere children were shouting and shoving in their usual gangs. Girls from 3B were playing tig and suddenly rushed towards her, darting in and out and round about. Her heart jumped and her satchel fell to the ground. They were going to ask her to join in.... But, just as suddenly, they tore off again. And she stood, her forehead creased into a frown. Then she crouched down and put her fingers round her satchel. She opened it as slowly as possible and counted her books. Her hands lingered over their covers, but finally she had to fasten it up again. She raised her eyes. There was no one left in her part of the playground. She humped her satchel onto her back and trailed across to the wall.'

I find that writing in scenes takes more words, more observation, and more subtlety. Adjectives are a luxury I rarely allow myself. There is no point if you are writing a novel, in saying 'a lonely child' or 'a solitary child'. Rather, show that child being lonely: no friends in the playground, a mouth that doesn't smile much. Indeed I might not use the adjectives 'lonely' or 'solitary' at all, but imply loneliness and solitariness through the scene and let the reader work it out.

In my Noel Proctor biography I wrote twenty-seven

thousand words in Part One. It was scene after scene of his early life, linked with the barest of narrative. Even as I was doing it I knew it was going to be too long. And indeed it was. Much of it was cut or implied in the pared down chapter four. Yet I had learned an important lesson. I *had* to sort out all that material and see it in its context before I knew what to cut out. I suspect most books are improved in the paring down process.

In order to tell Noel's story as I felt it should be told, I made a conscious effort to use the language of 'ordinary' people and not 'intellectual' language. To use words with an Anglo-Saxon root, that appeal widely. C. S. Lewis said,

> I aim chiefly at being idiomatic and racy, basing myself on Malory, Bunyan, and Morris, tho' without archaisms: and would usually prefer to use ten words, provided they are honest, native words and idiomatically ordered, than one 'literary' word.

One morning about three years ago I got a largish (for me) and unexpected cheque, and commission from a magazine editor. It was the first time I'd ever been paid for a piece of work and I was delighted. As I pondered this pleasant happening I realised it was almost seven years to the month from when I'd first begun to write in earnest. Seven years. The time a mediaeval apprentice was made to work with a Master Craftsman, until he was deemed fit to work alone and bear the name of craftsman for himself. For seven years he worked without pay. For seven years. I smiled to myself. I'd done my seven years apprenticeship and learned a lot. Now, perhaps at last, I could earn the name of writer.

The writer who is a Christian has a bonus. He knows the Creator and is consciously linked with him and his creativity. Christ is the Word, the Logos. In the ASB Prayer Book there is the phrase: 'He is our Living Word,' in one of the Communion Prayers. This phrase has layers of extra meaning for me. He, the living word who stalks with light behind and within our words on the paper. For in the end it is not so much the call to be a writer, nor who sees my name on the cover that counts. It's a call to follow him, for his sake, not for the writing's sake alone. He likes to be chosen as the first love. He is the beginning and ending of all our writing endeavour. And of all things.

So as Bill said, 'Your Christ is worth writing well for.'

References:

Harold Massingham, *Black Bull Guarding Apples* (Macmillan Poets 1965); *Frost-Gods* (Macmillan Poets 1971).
C. S. Lewis, quoted in Roger Lancelyn Green & Walter Hooper, *A Biography* (Collins 1974).

By the same author

AN UNFADING VISION

'At any moment an unsatisfying life may become once more a grand adventure if we will surrender it to God.'

Within weeks of reading these words by Dr Paul Tournier, Edward England found his life was changed. He was launched on a new career: discovering the adventure of books; the adventure of authors; the adventure of God.

A single conviction lies at the heart of this inspiring publishing adventure: 'The best books are God's books, and they are books that change lives.'

'We see these books in the shops. We buy them. We read them. We lend them. How many of us ask what lies behind their birth and presentation to the world? The story is a fascinating one.'

Lord Coggan

£1.75

published by

HODDER AND STOUGHTON